čáppa duovdagaččat

        voja voja nana nana

    leat nu čábbát ahte čuovggade

beautiful dwelling places

        voya voya nana nana

    they are so beautiful that they sparkle

            Johan Turi

THE ROCKS WILL ECHO OUR SORROW

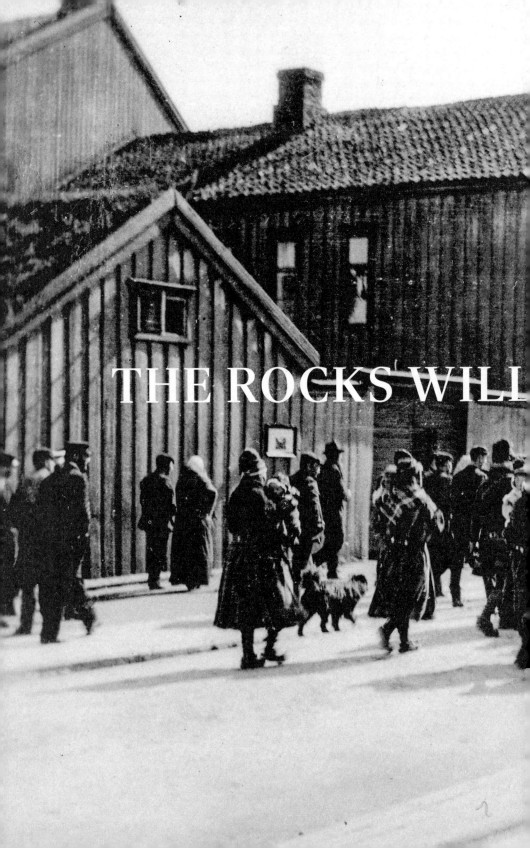

ELIN ANNA LABBA

ECHO OUR SORROW

UNIVERSITY OF MINNESOTA PRESS
MINNEAPOLIS
LONDON

MINNESOTA

The cost of this translation was supported by a subsidy from the Swedish Arts Council, gratefully acknowledged.

Note on the names of people and places: When more than one name is given, the first is the Sámi name (in nearly all cases in the North Sámi language) and the second (in parentheses) is the Swedish or Norwegian name. For example, Striima is the Sámi name for Strimasund (the Swedish name). Some names appear with different spellings (e.g., Arjeplog/Arjeploug); these reflect the spellings in the original documents.

Map by Jennifer Bergqvist

First published as *Herrarna satte oss hit: Om tvångsförflyttningarna i Sverige* by Norstedts Förlag, Sweden, 2020. Copyright Elin Anna Labba. This English translation was published by agreement with Norstedts Agency.

English translation copyright 2024 by Fiona Graham

Published by the University of Minnesota Press
111 Third Avenue South, Suite 290
Minneapolis, MN 55401-2520
http://www.upress.umn.edu

ISBN 978-1-5179-1330-4 (hc)

A Cataloging-in-Publication record for this book is available from the Library of Congress.

Printed in the United States of America on acid-free paper

The University of Minnesota is an equal-opportunity educator and employer.

31 30 29 28 27 26 25 24   10 9 8 7 6 5 4 3 2 1

eanan	the land
lea earálágán	is different
go das lea orron	when you have lived there
vánddardan	wandered
bivástuvvan	sweated
šuvččagan	frozen
oaidnán beaivvi	seen the sun
luoitime loktaneame	set rise
láhppome ihtime	disappear return
eanan lea earálágan	the land is different
go diehtá	when you know
dáppe	here are
máttut	roots
máddagat	ancestors

Nils-Aslak Valkeapää
Beaivi, áhčážan

Sážžá / Senj

Bådåddjo / Bodø

Gárasavvon / K

Giron / kiruna

Arjepluovve / Arjeplog

Gávtsjávrrie / Ammarnäs

striima / strimasund

Julevu / Luleå

Tråante / Trondheim

Staare / Östersund

Ubmeje / Umeå

Stuehkie / Stockholm

Romsa / Tromsö

Guovdageaidnu

do

Anaar / enare

hkkei / jokkmokk

murmansk

Contents

Snorgi

1

Bures eatnehat
First

The trail snakes up through dry bogs, disappearing, then reappearing. After a while it leads into sparse woodland where the birches
grow crooked. This is an old path; my body can sense it. I bear off at
an angle toward an opening farther on, tramping over marshland,
over the decaying trunks of fallen birch trees. I know the land
is returning to its original state; what I am looking for is barely
perceptible now.

I walk from one *goahti* site to another. The first lies at the top of a
rise, with a view out over the sea far below. It is so old that only the
fireplace remains. A patch of tall grass and a few overgrown stones.
Other sites are marked by soft rings where peat has subsided. I have
been here before and I know my way. I walk through an old reindeer
corral, passing a cold spring whose water is as clear as ever.

Never have I been in so silent a place. I can hear no wind, even
though I know it is blowing. It is a long time since the *goahtis* stood
here and children played between them. It is a long time since
anyone sat outside weaving, lit the fire in the *árran*, cut the sharp-
bladed sedge to line shoes.

The elders spoke of how they used to greet the land when they
came here, the mountains, the dwelling places, and the paths, but I
dare not. Just where do I belong? What is my home? I have discussed
this with other grandchildren of forcibly displaced people. What
part of our new Sámi herding grounds and settlements can we call

ours? I feel at home on the edge of this land, in places where I know nobody else longs to be, says one person. I don't feel very attached to the place where I live, says another. I can't say I'm unhappy here, but I lack a deep connection.

As the Finno-Sámi poet Áillohaš said, we carry our homes in our hearts. Can you do that if you were forced to leave?

Do I have the right to mourn for a place that has never been mine?

More than a hundred years have passed since the first forced relocations. That was when members of our family drove their reindeer over the strait to the mainland for the last time. The place where they lived has stood empty since. It is a place that whispers to those of us who know, who come here from time to time. But to most it means nothing. There is no awareness of the people who once lived here.

That is Sámi history. Tiny shifts in vegetation, a slightly raised patch of earth, *goahtis* razed to the ground. Our story is the plaque never erected, the chapter left out of the history books. Yet for some years now there have been court cases between the Sámi reindeer herding communities in the north and the Norwegian state. The Sámi communities are fighting for the right to the old reindeer pastures they were forced to leave behind. In Vapsten, in Swedish Västerbotten, families whose ancestors were established there before the relocations have sued the descendants of incomers. So there they are in court, fighting each other, prisoners of a history Sweden forced on them.

I lie down in the brushwood. It is only natural that the land should reclaim these places, but I am mourning for the story that is being obliterated as this happens. It is slipping out of my hands, and that is why I am here. My *váre,* my father's father, and his siblings lived here. And their parents, Risten and Gárena Jovnna.

2

This was their home. I wanted to start by writing about them but got nowhere. All I could find was a black-and-white photograph in a Helsinki archive, a picture of a mother with three young children. One of these children is *váre*, age ten. There are holes in the *gákti* he wears, and I know why nobody has mended it. The family is still in Gárasavvon (Karesuando), their winter home, in the middle of summer, when they should have been on the coast. They have been given a room in the district courthouse so they can stay with their gravely ill, bedridden *isá*. If the date given is correct, the picture was taken just after their father had passed away. "Paralysis following a stroke" the church register recorded as the cause of death. Risten, newly widowed, has so few reindeer that she can barely scratch out a living. Then the entire extended family is forced to relocate, and she puts her children in the *ráidu*. In 1923 they arrive in the mountains of Jåhkåmåhkke (Jokkmokk).

3

The time after that is a vacuum. They never wanted to talk about it. Now I know that my family is not the only one like this; the Sápmi where I grew up is full of people who have bound their wounds with silence.

So this will be a book about those whom I can write about, those whose recorded voices are preserved in archives and who were willing to tell their stories. Those with pictures, letters, poems, and documents. I am thankful for even the briefest of anecdotes and for what they have shared. In their history we can glimpse ours. Word by word, I write my own family back into existence.

Over the years I have interviewed many people, both those who experienced the forced displacements firsthand and their children and grandchildren. I was also given permission to use interviews recorded by others, all with elders long gone. This is a text based on a chorus of narrators: brief anecdotes, joiks, fragmentary memories. I have spliced and interwoven them: sometimes the colors are vibrant, sometimes the weave has holes and silence. Oral narratives have faded away over time. I have had to accept that the form of this text is necessarily like all Sámi history, like a woven *vuoddaga* severed by an axe. The threads have not even been torn apart; they simply come to an end, and the pattern is difficult to resume.

Along the way, those I interviewed have also begun to disappear, one by one. Each time it feels like losing a little of myself. Who are we to ask now? I have heard so many tales of forced displacement that need to be told by others. Not least the story of those displaced in their turn when the northern Sámi families moved onto their lands. I hope more people will tell their stories while there is still time. For many, recounting the tale is a way to heal. In the language I love best, to remember and to tell a story are almost the same word: *muitit* means to remember, and to tell or to recount is *muitalit*. We remember those whose story we retell.

4

Giitos eatnat. Thank you, *muore, váre, áhkku, áddjá*—my own and those of others. This is the web I weave for you. This is the joik I sing for you.

Rhvdnji

2

Rájit
Boundaries

Boundaries have always existed, but they used to follow the edges of marshes, valleys, forests, and mountain ranges. The new borders of the Nordic nations cut across all natural systems. They cut through pastureland, family ties, and transhumance routes that have been in use for thousands of years. When land is partitioned, people are separated. That is why an account of the forced displacements has to start precisely there. At the border, in 1751.

I would prefer this book to consist solely of people's stories, but it is hard to understand the forced displacements without speaking of the borders as well. The elders refer to them frequently, as these borders turned their whole lives upside down.

In 1751 the border between Norway/Denmark and Sweden/Finland is established. The Nordic countries and Russia split the territory between them and sign a border treaty. At the same time they deal with the Sámi, who have lived since time immemorial from the land, in a borderless region, by drawing up the Lapp Codicil, an addendum to the border treaty. This codicil acknowledges the Sámi as a separate people with rights over the land. It grants them the right to fish, hunt, and herd reindeer, as before. Every autumn, the reindeer herds migrate to their winter pastures inland. In spring, they return to the coast and their summer pastures. It goes without saying that the people, too, can cross the new border. But over time, the right to live as they have always lived comes to an end. During the nineteenth century, the borders are closed little by little, and the reindeer herds are forced into smaller areas. This process culminates in the early twentieth century, after Norway becomes an independent nation. Norway wants the land for its Norwegian citizens. People crossing the border with herds of reindeer are like a red rag to the Norwegian state. They don't belong to Norway, even though they have lived there for generations. The land where the reindeer graze is to be given over to saeters (mountain pastureland) or used to grow crops. "The nomadic way of life places a burden on the country and the settled population, and is hardly in keeping with the interests and the order of civilized society." These are the words of Labor Party leader Christian Holtermann Knudsen, spoken in the Norwegian Parliament, and he is not alone.

In 1919 Sweden and Norway resolve their common problem through a reindeer grazing convention that limits the number of reindeer allowed to cross the border. Indirectly, the two states determine at the same time how many people must be removed from their homes on the Atlantic seaboard.

From 1919 throughout the 1920s and the early 1930s, the Swedish County Administrative Boards resettle reindeer herders by force, to meet Sweden's obligations to its neighbor. The convention states that the relocations are to be carried out in line with the wishes "of the Lapp population." In reality, the people to be relocated have no say.

The authorities call this solution a dislocation.

In the Sámi language, this gives rise to a new word. *Bággojohtin*, forced displacement. Or *sirdolaččat*, as the older generation later call themselves, meaning "the displaced." The first ones to be forced out leave their homes with the belief that they will soon return.

Now I will hand it over to them, for they are the only ones who can tell the story.

8

"Let me tell you . . . That was the last summer we were there. No, it must have been the last spring . . . Márte Jovnna had a dream, which I can still remember: he dreamed that the Sámi traveled to the church in Tromsø. The reindeer herd circled around the church tower, again and again, until it collapsed. That was what he dreamed . . . He explained the dream to me, and he said, we won't be allowed to come here any longer now.

Then we got to know more about the convention, and we were told that we couldn't come back. *Sápmi* from Sweden can't come here any longer. It was the bailiff for Lapp affairs who told us that. The County Administrative Board traveled around like royalty, you know. Sweden was obliged to take in the Sámi.

And that was what happened."

Sunná Vulle Nihko Ovllá
Olof Petter Nilsson Päiviö

Norway has expressed the wish to reduce, as far as possible, the burden that the pasturage of Swedish reindeer places on the county concerned ... Sweden takes the view that the requisite reduction in the reindeer stock in the areas concerned could be achieved by having a number of Lapps and reindeer relocated from these areas to more southerly parts of the Lapp country in the county of Norrbotten, in accordance with the wishes of a section of the Lapp population of Karesuando and Jukkas-järvi. These areas lie principally in the parishes of Jokkmokk and Arjeplog, where it appears that there is sufficient room for the people concerned.

FROM THE 1919 REINDEER GRAZING CONVENTION

skåččås. En av de sista somrarna på selja

3

Mearráriikkas
In the Realm of the Sea

SÁŽŽÁ, SEPTEMBER 1919
Guhturomma Ánne Márjá
Anna Maria Omma

Ánne Márjá remembers. She remembers how the cuckoo called while they were on their way down to the sea. She heard it here and there along the way. It was as if it were following her. It didn't show itself; all it did was call out a greeting, a challenge, again and again. Each time it took her by surprise.

"The cuckoo calls whenever the fancy takes it," she thought. She looked around; it sounded so close but never appeared. When they reached the *goahti* at Várddaváraš it fell silent, and she forgot it for a while.

She remembers those summer sounds. The birds and the grunting, gangly reindeer calves. Autumn has a different tone, uneasier.

Ánne Márjá puts clothing into the bag and tightens the drawstring. Deftly she fits the more delicate china cups into her *gohppogisá,* while the medicine bottles go into the sack of flour. She and Guhtur have checked all the boxes they are going to pack. They have mended what needed mending, greased the leather straps and replaced those that were worn out. She knows just what she wants where; her hands think for themselves. The load mustn't exceed twenty kilos if the reindeer is to be able to carry it.

13

She needs no scales. Her arms know.

Gathering up the dry twigs that cover the floor of the *goahti*, she puts them on the fire outside. She paces back and forth with short, swift, bandy-legged steps. Ánne Márjá is like a ptarmigan, so the others say: her legs are as short and her movements as abrupt. She just can't walk slowly. The *boaššu* at the back of the *goahti* is nearly empty. There is a slightly musty odor of earth when the dry brushwood is gone. Breathing it in, she looks about her. Now all that's left are a few pots and pans, stacked upside down, and other things they usually leave behind. She picks up some twigs she dropped; she never goes empty-handed. Everything must be left clean for their return next summer. This is not a *goahti* for the unseen ones, the little folk.

The low mountains framing the valley are still quite bare. There's scarcely a patch of snow, though they're already in September. In a normal year, the mountaintops bear powdery shawls of new snow, but now all of them are still in summer's garb. Ánne Márjá's face grows warm. She hears the children by the stone outside the *goahti*. She sees the red bobble on her son's hat, bright in the midst of the brush, like an unripe cloudberry. She has sewn bells on little Ánne's and Heandarat's belts, so she can hear them tinkling if the children should wander off.

She pulls the crooked door shut.

Guhtur and Ánne Márjá's *goahti* is near the others in the *siida*. The other family groups live spread out over kilometers of hills around Várddaváraš. A few lonely mountain birches are dotted among the *goahtis*. The forest that grew here when Ánne Márjá was young has been cut down for timber. The valley is flecked with patches of bog in autumn colors, with dried-out cloudberry plants. Sedge that begins to turn yellow, blueberry plants, lady's mantle, wavy hairgrass.

They live on the threshold of the mountains, and if they climb the rounded slopes they can see the mainland on the other side of the fjord. They can see the sea, too; the open sea is no more than ten-odd kilometers away. Ánne Márjá thinks of these lands as sea and mountains in one, as if married to each other. Closing her eyes, she feels them within her. "The sea encircles the mountains and meets the next arm of the sea. We're surrounded by mountain peaks and sea. I've run about everywhere in these mountains. I know them well."

They call her Sážžá. She is so broad that they seldom think of her as an island. This is the land of their summers, the realm of the sea. Senja, as the Norwegians call her. Ánne Márjá is so familiar with the trail that she knows where it's driest to walk and which foot to set down on which tussock. In Sweden, her people are classed as Swedish citizens, and they have been christened by Swedish parsons. The forested land around Kangos lies on the Swedish side of the border. Ánne Márjá spends all her winters there but never feels a longing for the place. It's on the coast, on the Norwegian side of the border, that her worries disappear. Drawn to its summer slopes, Ánne Márjá is like the she-reindeer in spring; all of them raise their heads and face the wind from the coast. Guhtur selected the birch trees for their *goahti*. They asked the place for leave to sleep there in peace. It is Sážžá that readies Ánne Márjá for the coming winter. Only here does she feel she has time to spare.

When they arrived, Ánne Márjá and the other women borrowed a Singer sewing machine down in Rášmorvuovdi and made new *gáktis*. They tied down cattle hides in the lake and left them until the hair came loose. She has sewn summer shoes with tiny stitches and woven new *vuoddagat* for the children. She makes fine shoe bands; she's known for her skill. Once they've rounded up the reindeer from around the lake, she puts on freshly laundered clothes for the occasion. She has milked the most experienced she-reindeer, a few jets from each. "We made cheese, and *eidde* churned butter. That's what we lived on." It's hard when fresh, butter from reindeer milk, and white as snow. It melts like marrow in your mouth.

The cheese, the butter, everything they have: she's packed it all now. The summer passes so quickly. The *ráidus* are set to migrate from the summer pasture on the island over the border to Sweden. Ánne Márjá puts worn *dovgosat* on the back of the reindeer gelding. The hide protects him against the weight of the pack, and she places it hair side down to prevent the pack from slipping. Standing on the left side of the gelding, she tries to put his harness on without moving her upper body or taking overly long steps. She mustn't frighten him with quick movements. Singing a joik will calm him.

Ánne Márjá lifts Ánne onto the gelding she is going to lead herself; she knows he is the right one to carry the child. She sits the little girl down in an oblong case with rounded corners. It has a raised border, a hand's breadth, no more, but that is enough to support the two-year-old, who cannot really keep her balance otherwise. Heandarat is big enough to sit on the reindeer's back, holding tightly to the two parts of the *spagát* sticking up in front of him. She ties him on. He is braced on either side by cushions stuffed with reindeer hair. Whenever his legs start to feel numb, he dismounts and walks alongside the *ráidu* for a while, a pole in one hand.

Ánne Márjá was twenty-two when she became a mother: four years ago already. Just think, more than four years since she last migrated with the reindeer—she who had always accompanied the herd. She is tormented with longing when Elle takes her bag to go off foraging and she hears her sister's high-spirited joik. Ánne Márjá used to fly like a seabird over these valleys. Sometimes they would sit on a stone by the sea and joik: boys they had met and places they were fond of. They joiked the mountains. The maids from Ávkolat had fine, steady voices. When it is hard to move on, she thinks of the time when she was like a wild reindeer. "Guarding the meadows was really a task for farmhands and maids, but I was like a wild thing. I was always out there. I tried going to school, but time was too short. I never did anything but follow the reindeer, never. A joy, that's what it was."

Now she seldom leaves the valley. Sometimes she fetches fish from the fisherfolk down on the fjord. The last time she visited the farms in Rášmorvuovdi they gave her a syrup cake so fresh she had to wipe her knife before putting it back in her belt. "They're good people; they always have coffee and food. Oh, it's such a pleasure to drop in on them. Take a milk bottle down and they'll refill it for you. We've lived close to each other all our lives."

Well, well, that's all they're wont to say. They never make a big thing out of goodbyes; after all, they'll see each other again next spring. Making too much fuss over goodbyes bodes ill.

The *ráidu* makes its way down over several half-dried-out bogs, following the brook down to the ford. Ánne Márjá takes in the trees as she passes: roots, burr knots, birch bark. She thanks the trail, the slopes, the pastureland, the beck, which is quieter now. It is difficult to wade across the torrent in spring, but now it's easy enough to cross without getting the seam of her *gákti* wet. One of the channels is dry, its stones worn as smooth and round as pebbles on a shingle beach. Gripping the reins, she steers the *ráidu* up the steep bank. The reindeer's packs slide askew, are straightened. They catch up with the elders and the children, who had gone on ahead. The first leaves have been caught by the wind and blown on the trail.

The first leg of the journey isn't long. They're going only to Gibostad, as Norwegians call the farms around Čoalbmi. When Ánne Márjá was a child, there were only one or two houses here, but with each year that passes, new plowed fields appear beside the fjord. Their old fireplaces await them on a ridge at some distance from the nearest farm. She greets the site where they put up their *goahti*. It is in autumn apparel now; the last time they met was early summer. The foragers come to the cloudberry bog along with the reindeer herds.

Ánne Márjá meets acquaintances who have come a long way to fetch their reindeer for slaughter. The farm folk have come to trade goods for meat, hides, and blood. The fall reindeer slaughter is the high point of the year here. She registers her own reindeer. She knows them inside out, their antlers and their markings. Guhtur takes care of those that are to be slaughtered and sold. "Reindeer bulls are like horses," says her cousin Johánas, laughing. She checks whether any are missing; nobody wants to leave reindeer behind on the island. You can't be sure they'll still be there by next summer. There are far too many shotguns among the permanent island dwellers. Now their animals will encounter the bare mountains of the borders, and then the forests of their winter pastures.

Elle and three boys cross the strait in a rowboat to join the reindeer herd on the other side. The channel is so narrow that you can see the details of the houses on the mainland and the church where Lálle Jákos's son was buried. They wait for slack water, the time—barely an hour long—when the sea pauses between ebb and flood tide. The older reindeer dip their muzzles in the water. It is uncanny to see them sense the tide and lie down to wait. At slack water, they have the breathing space they need to cross the strait. In spring the reindeer are reluctant to cross, but it's easier now. The herd swims over, covering the fjord like a quilt, and races uphill on reaching the mainland. The farmer on the other side has put up barbed wire to keep them out, but they seem to get through anyway.

Ánne Márjá lights her pipe and inhales. The families are going to board the boat to Finnsnes, then reach the reindeer herd by horse and cart. There are other travelers on the broad wooden jetty, people in dark, drab clothes and hats. The older children help carry out sacks, *giissáid* and *spagát*. All the saddles and packing cases carried by the reindeer are to be taken across by boat now. As ever, their own place is outside, on deck. They sit down with their arms full of puppies and children.

From the sea they can see the reindeer trail and the mountains it follows. There is Noaddevárri; there are the slopes around Várddaváraš where the *goahtis* stand. *Vuoi,* these lands. The realm of the sea. The salt water. Ánne Márjá sweeps her woolen shawl about her, keeping Ánne warm in her arms. The women's white lace caps are bright in the sun. *Ipmil sivdit,* she thinks, may they fare well, until they see the realm of the sea next spring.

Only later does it occur to her that she might have said goodbye more affectionately. She should have spent longer with her friends in Rášmorvuovdi. Thanked them for the coffee, the coalfish, and the bottles of milk they had shared. For their conversations, their stories, and the time they'd spent together as children. And if they had known, they would have given away their belongings or sold them. She ought to have given thanks to each little path and to the cliffs of Juobmovári. She would have visited her father's grave.

Only later does Ánne Márjá remember that the cuckoo called more often than usual.

"The year they sent us away, that was the year the cuckoo called."

"She wanted to go back to Norway."

Did she ever talk about the forced displacements?

"No, she never mentioned the subject. It was as if she had repressed it."

Did she ever talk about Senja?

"All I knew was that they had lived in Norway. She rang Susanna and me and asked could we drive her to Norway, could I help her go back. When we couldn't help, she tried to get staff from the old people's home to take her there. She still had memories of the place. She waited for a chance to go home. Once she ran off, and they found her between Kåbdalis and Kitajaur. All loaded up, she was, with a walking pole. She waited until the lads were out working, then off she went. She never talked about it. She was just bent on going there."

To Norway?

"Yes, it was always Norway . . ."

What did she say?

"Just that she wanted to go home."

Sire Omma
granddaughter of Ánne Márjá Omma,
forcibly displaced in 1920

"Iŋgá siessá had a younger sister, Johanne siessá. One autumn, when they were about to leave Senja, Johanne wasn't well, so she stayed behind with relatives. Then came the ban that stopped them from returning to Senja. In 1920 they were ordered not to go back . . . They didn't know they wouldn't be allowed to return the next year, that's why they left Johanne behind. She was six. She lived with our relatives, who later became her foster parents. She was well looked after and later on she inherited her foster parents' house. It was only once she was grown up that she got in touch with her sister, and us . . . I went over to visit her and she treated me to those tasty fishcakes of hers.

Johanne's foster sister told me how Johanne sat behind the cow barn for several springs in a row. She'd sit there, waiting for them to come back and fetch her."

Lássbiet Heaikka Johánas
Johannes Marainen,
whose father's parents were forcibly displaced
from Sážžá in 1920

"A home is a home. Peat *goahtis* and goat huts and milking paddocks and migration routes. All the work they'd put in was left behind . . . It wasn't until they'd gone east to Gárasavvon that they were told, you won't be going back. Their homes were left empty, and rotted away. The earth took back their things. A small ring of peat was all that was left . . .

They'd talk about it whenever they got together . . . *dot riika.* 'The kingdom,' that was what they called Gárasavvon and the islands near Romsa. It was like a different country. But you know, they never really wanted to let anyone see them cry. Instead, they'd go up into the hills and wander about. They didn't want the children to see.

We didn't know anything about the old times, it was only when people came over from the other *goahtis,* when they met other people . . . then they'd talk about the past. They always told such fine stories. Their island had stayed in their memories as the most beautiful place on this earth.

We were out there once near Romsa with *eidde váidni* and Jovnna and Elle, and my mother gazed over at the island and really wanted to go there, but it didn't work out.

And so their memories disappeared."

Gátriina Lásse
Lars Jansson Nutti, whose parents
were forcibly displaced from Ráneš in 1919

A cleft in a stone contains broken marrowbones. Beside another stone, I find a rusty scrap of metal, greenish, rough to the touch—a discarded fragment of a copper pan?

I put it back carefully, as if it might crack. It might be a trace of those who once lived here. Could it have lain here ever since they were forced to leave?

There used to be more at one time, say those who have been here earlier: left-behind items. Schoolbooks from the summer school. Pots and pans and so on. Could there be things they had to abandon underneath the brushwood I'm standing on? Our family lived somewhere, but so far nobody has been able to say exactly where. They followed the reindeer here, until the moment when they were no longer allowed to stay.

The reindeer grazing convention that sparks the forced displacement of the Sámi is signed by the foreign ministers of Sweden and Norway on 5 February 1919. It comprises 202 paragraphs that enter into force in 1923, printed on fine paper and bound between covers the same mid-blue as the fabric of a *gákti*.

In the convention, Sweden and Norway agree to empty the reindeer pastures along the coast. They close off islands and peninsulas, and in other places nearer the border they limit reindeer numbers. The convention excludes reindeer herders from the seaboard to make room for agriculture. Sometimes they are referred to as "the plague of reindeer"—those reindeer that migrate annually to the coast. There is no place for reindeer husbandry, viewed as a dying practice; it is the livelihood of people regarded as a race on its way to extinction. Norway, now a new, independent country, has been seeking for some decades to rid itself of both the reindeer and the people who migrate with them. The country is to be Norwegian, and only Norwegian-speaking Norwegians are to live in Norway. Ivar Björklund, a professor of cultural studies, says this is essentially a question of social Darwinism. The Sámi are not viewed as having reached the same level of development as others. They are seen as archaic. "They were regarded as people who had nothing to do with us, as foreign nationals with a culture that was dying out. It was thought to be just a question of time until they disappeared anyway. Quite simply, they correspond to all the ideas about 'the other,' people who are different from us, who we want to distance ourselves from." Ivar Björklund notes that the Norwegian state already had all the instruments it needed to create that distance.

In February 1919, Swedish authorities move the first families. These are people who spend their summers near Soltunjávri on Ráneš, an island northwest of Tromsø. The move takes place just a week after the signing of the convention; the ink on the paper is barely dry. What are they to do with their *goahti*? Their storage buildings? Their reindeer corrals? Their family? Their friends? Will they ever meet again? Young couples make haste to marry, so they can move away together: mirthless shotgun weddings. They harness their pack reindeer in haste and are transferred initially to the Sámi reindeer herding community of Unna tjerusj, near Gällivare.

This all happens so fast that the authorities catch up with the formalities after the event. People have to sign documents applying for authorization once they have already arrived. The documents drawn up by the Lapp Authority leave a space for a signature, where they write their initials in a crabbed hand.

How much do they know about the convention? This is a legal text drafted in Norwegian and Swedish and translated into Finnish only later. It is never translated into Sámi, the language spoken in the region for thousands of years. Many people, like Ánne Márjá, have never been to school, and apart from Finnish and a little Norwegian they know only their own language. If they had understood what was happening, they would never have left children behind with relatives or simply abandoned their belongings. "We never had time to say goodbye," I hear many people say in interviews.

In the spring of 1920, several long *ráidus* are loaded up near Nearvá (Mertajärvi) and Gárasavvon (Karesuando). Seventy people are issued boilerplate letters of application to the municipalities of Jiellevárre (Gällivare), Jåhkåmåhkke (Jokkmokk), and Árjepluovve (Arjeplog). Ánne Márjá, Guhtur, and their children arrive in Tuorpon in 1920. I search for what she has to say about the journey but find only a few sentences, just like the scraps of metal I picked up. She, who laughs when reminiscing about their summer lands, does not want to recall their move. She says she dreamed of being able to visit her father's grave but never returned. Then she sighs on the tape, preferring to talk about something else. Her words peter out. Fortunately, others give a detailed account of the journey: the grazing land, the ice and snow underfoot along the way, the weather. The reindeer that resist the move. The animals are accustomed to migrating west in spring. Now the herders have to use all their strength to force them south, in the wrong direction.

Stockholm den 8 Februari 1923.

Nils jönsson Thithho

Barnens skildrat: ...

I recur

5 recur

Sanuo ...

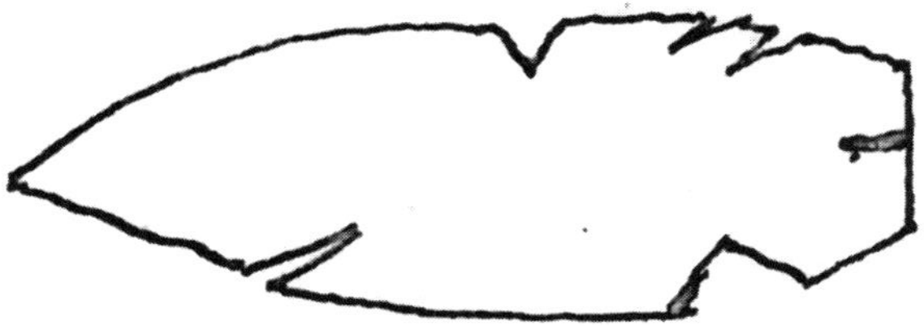

Datter Elli.

mánnga áhtte rilsá   mánnga áhtte Jorová

4

Gaskaija vuostá in vuolgge
I Will Not Travel toward Midnight

END OF FEBRUARY 1920
Márggu Ántte Jouná
Jon Andersson Blind

Jouná thrusts the pole down through the mantle of snow. It is
barely knee-deep. The ground is hard, frozen, but not icy. Up in the
mountains where it's been blustery there are dark patches of snow-
free ground. "That's fine grazing land, all right," he thinks. This is
the first winter in several years when the ground beneath the snow
hasn't been sheathed in ice.

Spring is likely to come early. Everyone says so. March is at hand,
márjábeaivmánnu, and it won't be long now till the sun begins
to spread its warmth. His sleep has been restless of late. Will the
ground hold firm throughout the journey? Will the spring overtake
them? They should have set off earlier.

They meant to start their journey a few weeks ago, in fact, but
postponed the *ráidus'* departure at the last moment. A baby boy was
born to Jouná's elder brother Nilsá and his wife, Gusttu Iŋgá, just
before Christmas. The baby was christened at home, and again by
the parson, but his name provided no protection. In early February,
lying in his cradle, he drew his last breath. Another little winter
baby. There was a sketchy question mark in the box marked "cause
of death" in the church register. The child was far from the first

infant the parson had seen die, but he was the first for Nilsá and Gusttu Iŋgá.

Jouná has kept the reindeer herd gathered together on a mountainside near Nearvá, and they have seen the other herds pass by. Jouná's uncle on his father's side, Márggu Biera, has already left. Gár Ántte Biera, Josvvá Biette, Bilttot, Guhturomma. They say the islands are empty now: all of Sážžá, and Ráneš, too. The people of Suolohasat have been dispatched, and there will be more to come. It's hard to know what's true. There's been so much speculation over the past year. Voices whispering, to keep it from the children.

Their elder brother, too, is all set to leave, but he changes his mind at the last moment. Now he's holding fire. And he is not alone, Jouná observes. "There's many supposed to be leaving who can't."

Taking out his big knife, Jouná scrapes snow off the lower part of the sleds. The thick fabric of the *goahti* is folded up and the tent poles lashed to a sled at the tail end of the *ráidu*. A sooty, slightly dented little coffee kettle is the last item they pack. Gusttu Iŋgá warms a smooth, round hearthstone found under a fallen pine. Pulling off her gloves, she checks that the stone isn't too hot before slipping it into the children's *roavgu*, a woolly sheepskin sewn at the foot end to form a sack. She lifts the children so that their feet rest on the warm stones, swaddles them, tucks them in, and cushions their heads with woolen shawls. Through the opening for their faces, you can see the mist of their breath. Tying her shawl about her shoulders, she fastens the draft reindeer's leather reins over its back and pushes her shoes into the ski bindings.

They move along, for longer stretches on some days and shorter on others, stopping where forage is available. The reindeer herds go first, with the *ráidu* following in their tracks. They have to go somewhere, after all. Exactly how far away seems to matter less to the Bailiff for Lapp Affairs than the fact that they are leaving. Just as long as they leave.

The bailiff, Mr. Holm, explained that everything is better farther south: "There is unoccupied land." He promised them fine pasturage for their reindeer. "There's room enough for herds of several thousand. You will be given all the help you need. Leave now, and you can choose your own land. But if you hold back, you'll lose that opportunity."

What is left for them if they stay? If they stay on, they'll probably be forced to leave sometime anyway. The first time the powers that be wanted them out of the way Jouná wasn't even born. He doesn't know anyone who has prospered in recent years. His own family has lost a third of their livestock in just a few years. Since the borders were closed, life has become increasingly unbearable. Their grazing lands have been overcrowded for too long, with too many reindeer and closed-off pasturage. You can scarcely touch the ground with an axe now. A few dozen kilometers to the south, a pack of twelve wolves has been hunting together. They have been breaking up the herds, isolating and separating the reindeer. One bellwether after another falls silent. "It's impossible to live here. There's not enough land for the Rosttu herds. The reindeer will die off." Jouná and Nilsá discussed matters during the winter and decide against trying to stay on.

The reindeer are grazing outside Vazáš, and the next day they continue their journey southward along the winter route toward Veaikevárri. The sleds grind over the snow. The trail hasn't been plowed, but the snow has been flattened by horse-drawn carts and reindeer hooves. Nilsá is always just where he's needed; when one man stops, the other takes over. They scarcely need to speak to each other. They know that if they lose the reindeer now, they might never find them again.

Both Jouná and his brother have the features of the Márggut clan, sharply delineated. Fair as mountain birches, with luxuriant mustaches. Jouná is a head taller and less vain than his brother. Jouná, like Nilsá, can strike up a *luohti* when he's in the forest, but he hasn't inherited Nilsá's love of joiking or his light voice. They were born into this life and bred to it, side by side. First they learned to slaughter calves, then full-grown animals. They would take turns to carry out the bones after meals and vie with each other over who was handiest with a lasso. They began to migrate with the reindeer herd as soon as they had the stamina for it. Their father kept a large herd, and their mother, Ánne, took care of their home when she was up and about. They learned to keep quiet about her illness. Ever since their birth, the light of spring has made Ánne ill. While others long for the sun, she trembles. She is having a hard time now, with the sun shining at full strength.

"It's as if the spring sunshine melts my heart," she'll say. "Any clear ideas run out of my head and down my backbone, into the very marrow." Ánne has remained alone since their father's death. There was no question of her staying behind, for who would look after her?

East of Giron they catch up with Márggu Biera, their father's brother, and his family. They have put up their *goahtis* beside a broad, snowy mire. The dogs yelp and someone swears at them to keep quiet. There are many people in their uncle's *siida*, and they are bound for the same place. They let their herds merge. As the *siidaisit*, their uncle has employed a guide. "I'm paying him out of my own pocket," he says. He isn't prepared to wait for the guides promised them by the Lapp Authority. Offers of help are no use if they never materialize.

They decide to buy provisions in Giron. There are traders in the mining town, and no one knows whether food is available where they are going. They harness reindeer to empty sleds and purchase provisions for a whole year: flour, coffee, sugar, tar. The *ráidus* are so heavily laden that they have enough to last until autumn at least.

The guide leads them to Gáláseatnu. "Keep going over the

mountains straight down to Gáidum," he says, pointing southward, and then Jouná watches him turn back.

The mountains in front of them are rounded, like the bottom of a wooden Sámi cup, but to the west frozen peaks point skyward. The traces of avalanches are visible from afar. They discuss where to stop. "This is like crawling headfirst into a sack," says Jouná. "We don't know a thing about the land where we're bound; we've never been there to see what it's like."

The reindeer herd spreads out as they move on. They travel during the early hours and sleep during the day. Every time they

stop for a rest, Márggu Biera skis on to see what lies ahead. On his
return, he tells them about the mountains that await them. The
only sounds along the way are the barking of dogs, the clopping
of hooves, and the creaking of skis. The dogs that need a rest lie
whining on the sleds. The children ask where they are going. They,
too, have begun to grasp that they are not heading home. From time
to time someone sings a *luohti*, but even the group of girls who are
fondest of joiking are unusually quiet. Márggu Biera's daughters,
Elle and Márge, and Gár Ántte Biret are always laughing and joiking,
especially when they are alongside the reindeer. They joik the
mountains when they are about to move on. They joik the people
they meet—but here nobody knows their names. No one knows the
notes for these lands. But each time they finish another leg of the
journey and let the herd free to graze, the girls joik with relief. They
have gotten through another day.

The sun softens the snow, and the night freezes it to a crust of
ice. The reindeer lie down to rest with their heads facing northwest.
When one gets to its feet and sets off toward the north, the whole
herd gets up. At night, they follow old reindeer that break loose.
Jouná keeps watch to the north. There's barely any need to watch
the area to the south; no reindeer are inclined to head in that direction. "We never let them out of our sight. But we do lose some—
bulls and older geldings, they wander off . . ." The females, too, turn
toward the northwest; the place where they usually calve lies five
hundred kilometers to the north. They can feel in their bones that
they are not where they should be.

After two months of travel they arrive at Mávas. The massif to
the west reminds them vaguely of the north. It is the first day of
May, and the sun hardly ever rests now; he disappears for barely an
hour or so at night. Jouná squints in the sharp, increasingly warm
light. His eyes sting in the snow mantle's glare. Though he has
pulled the peak of his cap down, it provides scant protection. They

put up the *goahtis*. Whose land is this? Is there enough forage for them to stop here? Maybe they can see the sea from those distant peaks, whose names he doesn't know.

Day by day they observe the mountains and the valleys, the land that is rapidly reappearing as the snow thaws. The patches of naked ground are sodden with meltwater, and the brooks are in full flow again. When it is Jouná's turn to rest, he dries the sedge lining his shoes by the fire inside the *goahti*.

Their mother fetches brushwood to keep the fire going. When she sits down, her *beaska* rides up in folds over her legs. Her face is deeply lined, tanned, and careworn. It must feel empty on her side of the *goahti*, yet she seldom speaks of Jouná's father. He was the very first to register for relocation. If he had been here now, Márggu Ánte, what would he have had to say? Jouná was twenty the first time his parents decided to move to new grazing land. Láhku could not provide for all the people living there. Leaving the district and their relatives there, they moved to Dápmotvuovdi. The borders were closed, and overcrowded lands have no future to offer. People can live only as long as their reindeer can survive, that was his father's view. The land must be able to sustain them. Jouná knows he no longer had any faith in a life in Rosttu.

"If you want a life with reindeer, you have to try to find better conditions, try to do better. That's how I see it."

If these lands will not take them in, he will travel farther. He fears nothing now. His whole body is restless; it's as if he is constantly on the move.

"A man who's left his lands no longer has a home. He no longer has his feet on the ground. That's how it feels to me. That man no longer belongs to the land."

Márggu Jouná will not look back. "I'll not travel toward midnight—I would rather walk on toward the day."

19**21** års **Utflyttningsbok**

1.	2.	3.	4.	5.	6.	7.	8.	9.	10.
Flyttnings-betygets löpande nummer	dag och månad	Utflytt-ningens år	dag och månad	Utflyttade. För- och tillnamn, yrke och näringsfång.	Födelseår, -dag och -månad	Mankön	Kvinkön	Varifrån i församlingen utflyttad.	Uppsi i förs lings boke
1	24/1	21	4/2	Nils Andersson Blind, fjällapp m. fam.	87 25/1	4	1	Könkämä	102
2	"	"	"	Per Olofsson Blind m. fam.	64 23/4	3	1	"	101
3	"	"	"	Elsa Persd.r Blind, lappd.r	98 12/2		1	"	"
4	"	"	"	Brita Maria Persd.r Blind "	99 16/9		1	"	"
5	"	"	"	Per Knut Persson Blind, lapp.	02 24/11	1		"	"
6	"	"	"	Jon Andersson Blind fjällapp	89 1/5	1		"	99
7	"	"	"	Per Lars Andersson punso, fjällapp, m. hru	83 9/1	1	1	"	114
8	"	"	"	Brita Andersd.r punso, lappd.r	97 3/6		1	"	"
9	"	"	"	Per Persson Kuhmunen fjällapp, m. fam.	80 17/4	2	1	"	117
10	7/3	21	7/3	Nils Zakarias Nilsson Omma, lapp m. fam.	80 6/9	2	3	"	129
11	7/3	"	8/3	Tomas Amasson Labba " m. fam.	77 29/3	3	2	"	120
12	7/3	"	8/3	Guttorm Guttormsson Omma m. fam.	87 29/6	2	2	Lainiovuoma	170
13	7/3	"	8/3	Per Jonsson Piltto " m. fam.	68 20/9	2	3	d:o	175
14	"	"	8/3	Henna Maria Omma f. Piltto, lappänka	52 18/11		1	d:o	170
15	22/4	"	29/4	Mariana Johansd.r Raeti f. Nutti, lapplinotn	96 20/11		1	Könkämä	125
16	9/11	"	14/11	Anna Karolina Olsson Surri, tjänarinna	04 7/5		1	Kyrkbyn	23
17	15/11	"	21/11	Josef David Ossian Engström, konstnär m. fam.	83 19/11	3	2	d:o	20
18	7/12	"	9/12	Johan Elis Hildasson, dräng	01 27/8	1		Mertajärvi	70
19	"	"	"	Johan Elis Pettersson Männui, dräng	02 3/12	1		Lainiovuoma	87
20	"	"	"	August Pettersson Männui, dräng	95 25/10	1		"	
21	"	"	"	Ellen Hildegard Johansson Nutti, flickebarn	18 25/2		1	Lainiovuoma	162
22	"	"	17/12	Lars Nilsson Holli, nomadlapp m. fam.	87 11/10	2	3	"	109
23	"	"	"	Gustaf Helmer Asplund Omma, lappdräng	04 6/12	1		Idivuoma	6
24	"	"	"	Per Mårtensson Nutti, nomadlapp	46 7/7	1		Könkämä	123
25	"	"	9/12	Maria Josefina Asplund, tjänarinna	97 17/6		1	Lisdaska	61

för *Karesuando* församling.

11.	12.	13.	14.
Varthän utflyttad		**Särskilda anteckningar**	Är, dag o. nummer, då detta om inflyttningen skedt.
Församling i län eller i stad.	Gård, gata och hus nummer o. s. v.		
Arjeplog		$316 \frac{74}{08}$	$21 \frac{16}{2}$
do			„
do			„
do			„
do			„
do		$346 \frac{74}{10}$	„
do		$311 \frac{74}{04}$	„
do			„
do		$46 \frac{197}{1901}$	„
Gällivare		$43 \frac{197}{1901}$	$21 \frac{2}{3}$
Jokkmokk			„
do		$319 \frac{74}{1908}$	„
do			„
do			„
Gällivare			$21 \frac{2}{5}$
Haparanda			$21 \frac{2}{5}$
Sollentuna		Frb	$21 \frac{27}{5}$
Wittangi	Soppero J. N. Kemen No 3	$542 \frac{74}{21}$	$21 \frac{18}{2}$
„	Soppero: Joh. Huinku.		„
„	„ Nath. Huinku		„
„	Lannavaara, Pag 63		„
Jokkmokk		$317 \frac{74}{08}$	$21 \frac{23}{12}$
„			„
„			„
Wittangi	Soppero, Pag 355		$21 \frac{18}{12}$

Were you forced to move?

"Yes, we were forced. There were so many people in Gárasavvon."

Was that a sad time?

"It was sad to begin with, yes, but once we arrived things went well. Of course, it's always sad to leave a country."

And to leave your friends behind?

"We left our friends behind and came here, where we saw Swedish people everywhere, though there were one or two Sámi here, too. There were Sámi in Virihávrre; in fact, they were relatives of ours. We came straight to Mávas, and there were two other families in the place where we ended up."

Could you understand each other?

"They spoke another kind of Sámi, and Swedish! So we couldn't understand a thing to begin with, but we did manage to learn."

Was it unfamiliar country?

"Unfamiliar country and unfamiliar people, but they were decent folk. They were good people all right."

Márggu Biera Elle
Elsa Omma, daughter of Márggu Biera,
forcibly relocated in 1920

In the course of the year, a very large number of the district's reindeer-herding Lapps have been transferred from their place of residence to other areas. The largest relocation was from Karesuando, but a few Lapps have also moved from Saarivuoma and Talma. The Lapps have willingly carried out these relocations (necessitated by the provision in the 1919 convention to the effect that far fewer reindeer may enter the county of Troms during the spring and summer), despite the many difficulties, the costs incurred and the losses associated with such a migration.

BAILIFF FOR LAPP AFFAIRS JOHAN OLOF HOLM, IN THE ANNUAL REPORT OF THE SWEDISH LAPP AUTHORITY, 1920

kjepluoris 1924

"It was a real caravan. Reindeer after reindeer . . . we arrived here in 1923. I was ten years old . . . In 1922 the County Governor came to Karesuando and told us when we were to leave. They had letters of application, they'd taken names. We weren't allowed to go to Kvaløya island . . . the Norwegians had vetoed that. The reindeer were spoiling their crops . . . the vegetation. That was off-limits. So the only option was to send us farther inland into Sweden.

And there was weeping and wailing . . . and religion. It was all the same to us, we were just children, but I was with Grandmother when she attended the prayer meetings in the fjords, and there'd be weeping and preaching about sin and blessings. It was terrible when you think about it! All the way, on the journey down here to the area around Kiruna and other places, they did nothing but weep and bid farewell to bushes and trees and stones . . . and the path they'd traveled along . . ."

Hurre Liisa Sára
Sara Harnesk, forcibly relocated to the
Sámi community of Sirges in 1923

41

In my own family, it was the family of my *áddja*, my mother's father, who were relocated by force. And that of my *váre*, my father's father. Every branch of my husband's family was forcibly displaced except that of his maternal grandmother. She fell in love with a man who had been forcibly resettled and moved south to be with him. Our children were born into a network of displaced families, with this history woven into their very sinews. They are growing up with other children who are nearly all from the same background. People who have been separated by force stick together over so many generations.

Like Jouná, my children belong to a lineage known as Márggut, the descendants of a matriarch named Márgu who migrated to Láhku on the Atlantic coast in the summers of the early twentieth century. Jouná sees reindeer calves being born for the first time on new land in 1920. Two years later, nearly everyone in his family, which is a large one, has been relocated. Only a thin branch of the family remains in the north.

I follow the displaced people on their way south, through digitized church registers. The church gave them names that sound more Swedish. Their papers refer to Jouná as Jon Andersson Blind. First they come to Mávas in the mountains of Árjepluovve, where displaced people account for half the church register. The names are alike; relatives travel together. In time, Márgu's children and grandchildren are dispersed, as if by the wind, throughout Sápmi. Branches are split, family trees uprooted. When these families are separated, many people lose the only protection they have. The network of cousins, godparents, and elders provides support in harsh everyday life. Family ties are the most precious thing anyone can have, apart from reindeer.

Jouná is one of the few who choose to relocate. When he arrives, he feels he has been taken in by *"guoros lohpádusat"*—empty promises. The pastures supposedly available for them farther south are already in other hands. There is no room for thousands of reindeer, as promised by the Lapp bailiff. Other reindeer are on their new land, and the reindeer herders they meet have opposed the influx of more people and animals. Newspaper cuttings, letters, and official documents show how conflicts grow in parallel with the forced displacements. There are smoldering conflicts between those forced to move south and those who have never asked for other reindeer herders to share their pastures (and who, in some cases, didn't even know that was going to happen). As early as 1922, the Lapp Authority writes that "the dislocation has resulted in disturbances and disruption, as the reindeer husbandry practices of the Karesuando Lapps are fundamentally different from those of the original inhabitants."

Jouná's name also appears in a letter in which he thanks the authorities for a relocation grant. He says he would never have thanked them, as he's never received any money. "That's something the Lapp bailiff cooked up himself—he thanked them on his own behalf. Someone wrote my name in the letter."

Are there other documents in their names of which they know nothing?

The new reindeer grazing convention enters into force in 1923. Then comes the year of large-scale relocation. The convention takes effect, and islands and peninsulas on the Atlantic coast are vacated. The authorities are in a hurry to send people on their way. The Lapp Authority is busy both forcing people to leave and pretending they have left of their own free will. Officials travel around "to process the Lapps." All the applications for authorization to relocate are virtually identical, with the same wording and written in the same style. They differ only in the names and signatures they bear. When historian Johannes Marainen gives talks on the forced displacements, he points out that few people even knew how to write and that his own relatives "almost certainly hadn't a clue about what they were signing."

The Lapp Authority now decides that those who relocate must receive some form of compensation. They pay out between 300 and 500 Swedish kronor retroactively to those who have already moved.

In the Sámi communities of the north, unease spreads through the *goahtis*; it dwells in their fabric, the brushwood, and the *asttahát* used to stir embers. Who is being forced to leave? Who is permitted to stay? Those forced to leave now know that the move is final and that they will never return. Throughout their journey, they thank the places that have been theirs. They say *hivás de ealli ja jámet:* farewell to living and dead alike. They give away their belongings, everything they cannot take with them.

Their names are passed on to the church, which deletes the names of people from the Sámi communities of the north and sends them to the pastors farther south. In 1923 they are registered in localities in Norrbotten that have been selected by the Lapp Authority. That spring, 120 people are forced to travel south with their reindeer. Some cover nearly six hundred kilometers on the way.

Till Skötsörkiga och Högaktade vederbörande myndigheter har vi undertecknade
genom vår Högaktade lappfogden Oxerberg,
framför a våraen af Hjertad utgående Tack-
till de myndigheter som då älskat oss från
Karusuande, Till Arjepleog inflyttade nordna
der bidragit och skänkl oss Kontanta medel
hvilcket vi undertecknade mottagit genom
lappfogden Claus Oxerberg.

Per Olsson Blind   Mahasvahne
    P. O. B.
Nils Andersson Blind.   do
    N. A. B
Per Persson Kehmonen   do
    P. P. K.
Peter Suovo   do
    P A J
Jonas Andersson Blind   do
    J. A. B
Jon Olsson Blind   Semisjaur
    J. O. B
Olof Olofsson Blind   do
    O. O. B
Anders Andersson Blind   do
    A A B

        Arjepleog, den 11/2 1923.

Sirkkis, Sirkkis

Šiellajuovas Sárgávárrái
Dielbmačohskas Suddásii
Sápmelaččat soabalaččat
sirdolaččat sierralažžii
Ultivačča oarjeravddas
ovdasámit álddu bohče
Sirdolaččat Váisáluovttas
stuorra čuovžža basadedje

From Šiellajuovva to Sárgávárri
From Dielbmačohkka to Suttis
peaceful Sámi
migrants scattered
from the south side of Ulldevis
the Sámi leading the herd milk a reindeer cow
Migrants from Váisáluokta
cook a great whitefish over an open fire

Norgga vuosttá, Norgga láibbi
doaresnoðiin guottadedje
Leibbogárddis mielkki bohče
gieresráidduin luksa johte

Suorvvá dámmes, ruovdeskearuin
stuora muorkkis losses geasus

Sáltoorddas sierra ealuin
siidagaskkaid čorastalle
Ultivačča birra, birra
Borga láhpiha sámi láhtu
geaðggi duohkái galbmon čoahkkái

Norwegian cheese, Norwegian bread
they pack in saddlebags
in the corral they milk
with a string of reindeer sleds they travel southward

At Suorvadámmen with iron carts
at Stuorra muorki the going gets arduous

From the tree line at Sálto with herds separated
small flocks of reindeer pass between *siidas*
around and around Ulldevis
falling snow covers the tracks
of a Sámi frozen behind a rock

—Paulus Utsi

Translated by Thomas A. DuBois
and Harald Gaski

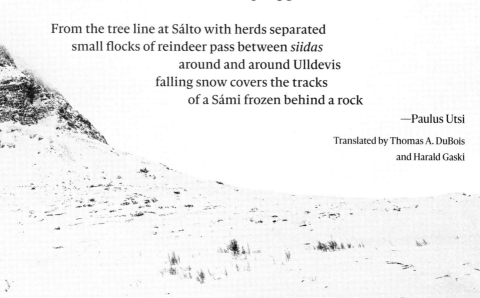

5

Goahtoeanan, báze dearván
Farewell, My Homeland

APRIL 1923
Dillá-muore
Margareta Utsi

Dillá has slackened her belt little by little as necessary. She can't loosen it completely, as that would let in the cold spring air. But for the time being she can adjust it so that it either rests above or hangs just below her belly. The generous cut of her fur tunic accommodates her growing girth. Though never particularly slim, even as a girl, Dillá found that her body would readjust after the birth of each of her first few children. But not any longer. She's long since altered the *gákti* she wore when she met Mihkel Biera. Not that it worries her: she's come to terms with her appearance. She does miss the lightness of foot she once had, though, and the energy to keep going. As her shoes sink into the cold snow, she tries to focus on the child she's carrying. Maybe it will be a girl this time? A little girl after her seven sons. If not, it will be another boy to work with the reindeer.

Seventeen years separate their eldest son from the unborn child she carries. She has had her children at regular intervals, as if by a mathematical formula, with two years between births. Their youngest children travel in the sleds making up the *ráidu*, while the two eldest, adolescents now, help out with the reindeer. They have

49

been following the herd on skis ever since the family started their journey from the north.

Their sixteen sleds weave across the bare uplands, following in the herd's tracks. They have been making their way southward since *gintalbeaivi* at the beginning of February, and now it's already April. They travel toward the light as daybreak approaches, resting in the middle of the day when the sun is at its zenith. There shouldn't be long to wait now.

On the way down from the mountains lies a frozen lake the shape of a belt, embedded among the hills. Lofty peaks greet them to the west. On the southern slopes their *ráidu* passes naked land emerging from melting snow. Dillá's eldest son, Biette, has accompanied the reindeer herd ever since they left Nearvá. Looking out over the spring flatlands, he says: "It's like a spring paradise. Holes in the ice and bare patches where the snow's melted . . . It's the best place I've ever laid eyes on." Dillá has never seen such good grazing land either. No sooner do they halt than the reindeer start digging. They had a problem with the herd only once, the night the wolf made off with six reindeer. One of the females belonged to Mihkel Biera. If it hadn't been for Olá, the hired hand, they would have lost more. "That'll be the old wolf from Duibi," said the ptarmigan hunter they met among the *goahtis* up in the mountains. Luckily it hadn't had enough time to scatter the herd.

The elders talk things over: should they stay here over Easter and let the reindeer graze? They have Válkko, Heaikas Lásse, the Báluhat family, and other families both ahead of and behind them, but everyone is just the right distance from each other. They don't yet know what's coming: maybe some of them will end up on the same land.

Biette attended last winter's meeting in Gárasavvon together with his father. The Lapp bailiff had convened a meeting in the courthouse, a timber building not far from the church. Nearly all of the *siida* leaders from Rostu were there, dressed in furs. Moisture trickled down the damp inner walls; the air was cold. Holm, the man they called "*sundi*," was there: the mustachioed Lapp bailiff with pale eyes, in his double-breasted felt jacket. For all his regal demeanor, what he knew of reindeer husbandry came entirely from books. "Tough decisions are made, and they read out the names of the people who are to leave. I hear them read out *isá*'s name."

Biette hears others say they're not going anywhere. But if their land has been declared off-limits, where are they supposed to go? Many purse their lips, looking neither right nor left. "*Sundi*" takes the floor again, speaking Swedish. Only later does Biette grasp what he announced. "They decided we had to go somewhere else. There was nothing to do but leave."

By the time they emerged from the meeting, darkness had already fallen. All that could be seen was the glow from the sparse windows of the chimneyless cottages and a sprinkling of lights on the other side of the river, a hundred meters away, in the part of the village that now belonged to Finland. In all the *goahtis* and bakehouses, people were talking about the same thing. Does anyone know the country they are being sent to? What kind of country is it? Are the reindeer different there?

Nothing had any taste to it now: neither sleep nor the food they ate.

They were issued typewritten letters requesting authorization to relocate. It felt as if the very paper these were written on might fall apart when they signed. "An act of intimidation," according to Biette.

Dillá tries to work as fast as she can. They cover the bare *goahti* poles with thick wadmal fabric. Firewood is carried in. The youngest children remain seated in the sleds, waiting. She knows it won't be long before they start crying. Dillá's younger sister, Elle, puts up her *goahti* next to theirs; the Ánddirat family occupy a third one. Elle's husband, Adjá Biette, rises before the sun awakes to take over from the hired man who has been watching over the reindeer. They help each other, sharing the workload. There's always someone on hand to give the children a bit of jerky to suck or to help any toddlers who need to pee while the *goahtis* are being put up. Soon smoke rises from the *reahpen* and the first coffee pot is simmering. The youngest children go out like a light the moment they have been fed.

Making your own choices in life isn't a given. You have to be thankful for what you have. Marry quickly if that will give you a chance of a good life, especially if your intended is a reindeer owner. Dillá listened to her elders' counsel. When she and Mihkel Biera wed, she was already with child. Mihkel Biera was tall and good-looking, and Dillá was a maid of all work. They married hastily in midsummer, when her *gákti* still concealed her growing belly. Mihkel Biera is twenty-four years Dillá's senior, old enough to be her father. He's been married twice before and has lost six children and two wives before her. When he and Dillá started sharing a *goahti*, he brought his youngest daughter home. Dillá mothered both Mihkel Biera's daughters and their own sons. All her children have run about in the summering grounds by the fjord. They've slept on the brushwood floor of the *goahti*, under *rákkas*, flown fleet-footed along the trails, with the tang of the sea air all around them. The child she now bears will be born into a new world—if it lives.

She's been lucky so far. Nearly all her children have survived. She lost her firstborn daughter, Susánná, one of a pair of twins. A year or so later she also lost the little boy they had christened Johannes, who had been with them for barely two years. She knows many mothers who have had heavier burdens to bear. They have learned not to talk too much about the life to come. They carry logs through to the right place in the *goahti*. Dillá conceals her belly so it can grow in peace: she mustn't attract ill luck or take fright if it can be avoided. The other women lend a hand without passing comment. Their tacit, sometimes involuntary sisterhood keeps them going when babies born in the *goahtis* in the cold of winter die before the sun returns. The names of the dead are passed on to the children who come after them. The soul passes on: it returns. There is some consolation in that thought.

A kilometer or so farther south they come upon a mature forest. Ádjá Biette and Ánddir *áddjá* apply a fresh coat of pine tar to their skis. According to the guides' instructions, they should soon reach their destination. They go ahead to scout out the lay of the land, as they need to know where they are heading. Never have they seen such tall trees: their trunks corkscrew skyward, and silvery-gray pine snags lie felled by the wind. Up in the north, the pines are so sparse that there are scarcely enough for them to tether their pack reindeer. Here, the forest is dotted with thawed patches a meter or more across. A little farther down, the woods meet a broad expanse of lake—Lulajávri, perhaps?

To the west, they hear a dull, metallic thudding that comes not from the land but from heavily laden horse-drawn carts crossing an ice-bound lake. None of the travelers understand Ánddir *áddjá* when he attempts to communicate in Norwegian, but he gets through to them with gestures and finds someone he can talk to, as he always does.

"We're taking provisions and materials to Suorvvá, where they're building a dam," says the man in his lilting dialect. "This is the Lule River lake system."

"Can we buy food around here?" asks Ánddir *áddjá*.

"Yes—there's no store nearby, but you'll always find food."

The children keep a lookout and call out when they come. Everyone gathers to share the news. Bietta hears them talking about horses that pull carts and people who holler while they work and speak only Swedish. "We've found the right spot for crossing Lake Lulajávri. We know where we're going now." Ádjá Biette gathers the children together. "There are trees as big as giants in this land. And trees with berries!" They grasp that this really is a different country.

A few days later they continue their journey up the slopes of Juobmo. The sweat pours off them as they urge the reindeer over the land where the snow has already melted, driving them onward and upward. The *ráidus* strain and tip over, weighed down with meat to last the spring and summer, gunnysacks full of flour, salt pouches, and ten-kilo sacks of sugar and coffee beans. They also carry stewing pans, summer clothes, and boxes containing silver and other valuables. Never before has Dillá led such a heavily laden *ráidu*. They swap the pack reindeer around so that those that have worked hard get lighter loads next time. Back home, it's their custom to leave provisions in the places they know they'll always return to. But this *ráidu* is loaded down with uncertainty.

Before their departure, the local storekeeper sold off everything he could to them. "After all, you don't know what there is where you're going." Some bought eight hundred kilos of flour, one hundred kilos of coffee. And pine tar—far more than they should have bought, given the need to spare the reindeer. Dillá and Mihkel Biera were handed 500 kronor in a brown paper bag, by way of a travel allowance. It looked like a lot of cash, but what they bought in Giron took a sizeable bite out of it.

After they guide the herd over the slippery ice of another lake, they head up into the mountains. Lapp Inspector Enbom is waiting for them at Sáltoluokta. He leafs through a notebook in search of their names: all of them are on his list. Mihkel Biera and Dillá's papers say they are bound for Ulldevis, but Enbom redirects them: "You're to go to Vájsáluokta." He sends the others to Mávas, Viri-hávrre, Guvtjárre, and Låddejåhkå. "He's like a parent giving his children instructions," Biette observes. He recalls the first time the Lapp bailiff told his parents to apply for authorization to relocate—those fine words about the good life supposedly awaiting them. "You've such a large family, man. So many sons." The officials told Mihkel Biera he should think about his children's future.

Dillá stays down by the lake. While the children play, she packs Lásse's belongings, putting in woolen shoe bands she has woven herself. She wove them specially for him, thread by thread. Elle asked if one of Dillá's sons could go to Árjepluovve with her to give her a hand on the journey. Dillá and Mihkel Biera have so many boys to look after. Dillá promised her sister that Lásse could go with them as an *unna reaŋga*, a young hired lad. He's nine years old: he can help with the *ráidu* and look after the little ones.

    Dillá and Elle pack together. When Elle's sleds are about to set off southward, they direct Lásse to his aunt's *geres* before it moves off, away from his own family. Lásse, the skinny, grave nine-year-old who has shot up like a beanstalk. Dillá doesn't know when she'll be able to bring him home. She repeats to herself that he will be well cared for where he's going, as if praying for the soul of a loved one on a religious feast day. He'll be well cared for. They take their leave swiftly. There are no words that can soothe the pain.

Dillá and Mihkel Biera head west. The hired men and the older lads split up. They separate the cows from the rest of the herd to give them peace and quiet before calving, and they move the bulls to another mountainside. They watch over the herds, each on his own: night, day, and night.

It is midsummer when Dillá first sees her new summer dwelling place on the shores of a lake: low land with promontories and inlets. The long scree slope of the mountain overlooking the lake casts a shadow over the land early in the day. Tentative young birch leaves shimmer like newly burnished silver. To the east of a river in full flow, glacier-clad peaks stand straight-backed.

Near the lake, a boat that's been dragged inland lies topsy-turvy; the boys take it down to the shore. They undo their shoes and wade across the flooded terrain. The dammed-up water makes for late spring floods, midway through early summer. They row out on the lake with clumsy strokes. Although they have grown up on the coast, they never had a boat, just fished in mountain lakes with lines and hooks.

Dillá walks about, taking in her surroundings. She's looking for springs and useful stones. The smell is different here. No salt water, no seaweed: instead, there's an odor of last year's withered leaves and the scraps of mold left when the blanket of snow melted away.

The children romp about, shooting off into trees and up mountain slopes. Dillá patches worn-out leather soles and weaves shoe bands for everyday use. A pipe dangles from her mouth, and she wears her cap pulled low over her forehead, covering her dark hair. She feels more and more ungainly as time passes, and her gait is now a heavy waddle. The other women keep an eye on her, never leaving her alone for very long. She barely sets eyes on Mihkel Biera. The men are marking the calves up in the mountains and keeping watch day and night over the herds. They are so afraid of losing them. Their reindeer are used to swimming in the sea, and if the men don't keep

watch over the headlands around the lake, the animals will set off
northward and be lost to them.

Dillá misses Elle. She wonders how Lásse is faring, how he's
doing where he is now, so far away. Is he using the shoe bands she
wove? She needs to prepare for giving birth and to arrange for help.
Someone mentioned that Bártta Elle has the necessary skills: she
has experience with attending births and looking after sick children.
Dillá borrows a boat and gets someone to help her row. She has to
cover thirty kilometers along the lake as well as some distance on
foot after that.

At the end of August, lying beneath a *rákkas* in one of the *goahtis*
in Läjbba, Dillá gives birth to a baby boy. She tucks the little one into
the cradle she's brought with her, swaddling him in calfskin bedded
on moss. Making sure his head is supported, she tucks the calfskin
over him and laces it up. There wasn't to be a new little Susánná, so
she leaves the bindings on the cradle unchanged. The baby is Olá
Johannes: Johannes after the brother who died. He'll be her and
Mihkel Biera's *váhkar,* their youngest child, who will take care of
them one day. He has a silver button to shield him from evil of any
kind and to protect him on the journey to the forestlands, which is
drawing nearer. New fall pastures and new winter grazing land. She

needs to rest now. For her own sake, this baby should be her last. Her body can't take any more.

Though Dillá rarely goes out, people come to visit her. She takes pleasure in offering them food and coffee. The women from the other *goahtis* sometimes turn up with sinews threaded through their belts, which they braid as they talk. They pull out needles from the needle cases suspended from their belts and chat while their hands fly. The talk is of the people living in this new land: their plain, dull-colored *gáktis*, adorned with straight bands. The peaked caps they wear, Swedish style. The way they vault over streams with long poles, flying just like sparrows. Their reindeer are crow-black, like soot, and as tame as goats.

They talk about *min riika*, our land—the land they've left behind, so different from *dát riika*, this land. They talk about religious feast days in Gárasavvon, about their kinfolk and the coastlands. About borders, reindeer police, and fines. The tutelage of the Lapp bailiff. One of the women is sure they have come to a land of bears. There are cairns of scree. Predators' lairs. It's so stony that you don't even know where to sit down.

All that matters, Dillá thinks, is that her sons can get by. It would be good if they could marry into wealth, she says in jest, but she means it. She must make sure they can get by. Mihkel Biera says the reindeer are grazing as if rooted to the spot. At least the grazing land gives no cause for complaint. If these lands can provide food and a livelihood for all her boys, she'll be content to make her home here. As long as her children can get by here, she'll not mourn for her old home.

58

"In our *goahti* it was nothing but work, work, work . . .
They didn't talk. I don't remember if we ever spoke about
our feelings. I never learned the words you need to talk
about such things . . ."

Can you recall anything they said?

"I remember Dette-*muore* . . . She was a widow who lived
with us some of the time and traveled with the family
when we moved from one place to another. I remember
one time when Dette-*muore* thought she was alone. We
had a very big *goahti*, and her sight was very poor, so she
didn't see me. She was sitting there, and I don't know
whether she was joiking or murmuring to herself or
telling a story, but she was reminiscing about the places
where she'd once lived . . . in the summer months. She was
stroking her coffee pot, murmuring 'my mother's coffee
pot, our hearth. Min riika.' Norway and Gárasavvon, that
was 'min riika'—our land. Those lands far away, that was
what she had on her mind."

Uhci Biette Iŋgir
Inger Juuso, granddaughter of Dillá-*muore*,
forcibly relocated to the Sámi herding community of Sirges in 1923

"They'd joik whenever they met and while they were out among the reindeer. Whenever they saw a reindeer they'd start to joik . . . Joiking was just part of life, you could say. It's part of the way you work . . . When there's a special feeling in your heart, you have to joik.

But I don't know if they had a joik for these mountains. Did they joik here at all . . . I've never heard that they did. Everything was unfamiliar. They'd joik a mountain peak here or there, I'm sure. They'd joik a person now and then. But you know, when you've been driven out of your own land, where your parents and your ancestors grew up, everything seems alien. This place is a haunt of wolverines, they used to say. It's so rocky, there's so much rock everywhere . . . The old *ádját* called it the lair of the wolverine."

Sunná Vulle Nihko Heaika
Henrik Päiviö

60

As of 1923, the new reindeer grazing convention between Sweden and Norway entered into force and its provisions began to be implemented. The many new provisions laid down in the convention, especially the new division into more reindeer grazing districts of a smaller size, and the ban on using certain previously legal reindeer grazing areas in the counties of Troms and Nordland, gave rise to serious concerns about its possible impact on the Lapps in the first year. All reindeer grazing is now prohibited in a very large part of the area where reindeer pasturage was formerly legal.

FROM THE ANNUAL REPORT OF THE SWEDISH
LAPP AUTHORITY, 1923

The hide hanging on the wall is molting, while the cushion is starting to gather mold. A musty smell spreads through the *goahti*. The picture on the wall is crinkly with damp. The pots and pans rust once the roof has given way, letting the rain in. Once the birds and other creatures see that no smoke ever rises from the *reahpen*, they make the dwelling their own.

These abandoned homes can be found all the way down the coast of Troms county after 1923. There are deserted *goahtis*, corrals, and storehouses in places such as Stállonjárga, Málatmuoki, and Rávdnjevággi. Some of the permanent residents feared the old, abandoned "Lapp camps," believing them to be haunted. The *goahtis* highest up in the settlement where my family lived are burned down in the year that the convention takes effect. On Ráneš, farther north, the pragmatic local landowner dismantles the corrals and uses the timber as firewood.

They say that those who were forced to leave joiked constantly that year. Joiks of mourning for the land.

There should also be joiks to their dwelling places. Although I know there are joiks to Stuoranjárga and Vinjevuopmi, I haven't been able to find any others. Would they have continued to joik if they had been allowed to stay?

Would I have had the chance to learn?

Artist Maj-Lis Skaltje, who has written about and made films about joiking, believes that many *luohtis* disappeared with the forced displacements. "When you're forced to leave an area, the joiks that belong to it are also left behind."

62

Very few people took their joiks with them. One of the consequences of the forced displacements was that the joiks fell silent.

In the stories I listen to from the time before the displacements, people joik when they meet the mountains. They joik in greeting and when taking their leave.

They give thanks for the pasture, the summer, the wind.

They ask the land for its permission.

They have a story and a name for even the tiniest little brook.

Everyone knows that reindeer herding demands a close relationship with the land and a knowledge of its smallest features. Everyone knows that those who migrate from one place to another aren't rootless; they just travel between different homes.

The way the Swedish authorities interpret the word "nomad" is based on a stark contrast. Since, by definition, nomads are people who travel around, the authorities think they can simply be moved from one place to another. "Obviously, they thought it was easier to displace Sámi reindeer herders than settled farmers," says Patrik Lantto, a history professor who has studied the Swedish Lapp Authority as an organization. In the 1920s, the Sámi are viewed as a single, homogenous group. Reindeer herders are reindeer herders, no matter where they live. In the eyes of officialdom, it matters little which Sámi herding community they belong to.

When the forced relocations are carried out, Sweden's attitudes tally with those of Norway, which has been making strenuous efforts since the mid-nineteenth century to cut back reindeer husbandry. Norway's official stance in the early twentieth century is that reindeer herding is destined to die out. Everyone in Norway must undergo Norwegianization and speak Norwegian. Reindeer herders are an anachronism in the new Norwegian nation, even more so if they spend the winter in Sweden or Finland. They have no place in Norway, and they are to disappear. The question of where they are to go is not the Norwegian state's problem.

The displacements might have stopped in 1923, after the authorities had sent off the people they had agreed with Norway to move. But shortly after the first wave of departures, there is a dramatic increase in reindeer numbers. The 1920s see good, dry winters, good grazing and growth. There is a light covering of snow and the reindeer calves live to see another year. The young survive the winter. Even though thousands of reindeer have been driven southward from the Sámi herding communities of the far north, there are soon just as many again. The authorities recognize that further forced displacements will be necessary.

As yet, those families who are still allowed to migrate to the Atlantic seaboard with their reindeer know nothing of the next planned "dislocation." They plan for the future—as if they still had one in the far north.

Bávlos

Bielle   Ándde   Lásse

Mihkel Biera   Mihkkal   Jovnna   Nigá   Dillá

Dat stuor'hearggit

Stuor'njárgga stuor'hearggit

stuorrát dego heasttat
ja lojit

Those big reindeer geldings,

big geldings of Stuor'njárga

as big as horses
and tame

Andon ovllá beatnagiin

6

Stuoranjárga
The Last Summer but One

AUGUST 1924
Ándom Ovllá ja Mihkel Biera Ristiinná
Olof Andersson Omma and Kristina Omma

The Stuoranjárga joik about the big geldings, draft reindeer the size of horses, is known far and wide. It's been familiar to Ándom Ovllá since early childhood: the joik about how the geldings graze and graze on pastureland that never ends. This joik comes to them sometimes while they're rounding up their animals and keeping watch over them. Especially on fine days when the reindeer are foraging high on the mountainside, when there's wind and sun and the calves are growing steadily. At such times they joik her, Stuoranjárga, the peninsula jutting out into the sea.

When the clouds drift over, silence falls upon the land. On the days when clouds hang heavy over the mountain peaks, the joik to Stuoranjárga is not to be heard. It dies away with the arrival of the *skoaddu*, as the people of the coast call the fog that blankets the peninsula like a woolen *rátnu*. It is a fog that drives reindeer from the mountainsides, down to the fjords. When Ándom Ovllá observes signs of low pressure, he's quick to pull his shoes on. He knows the clouds mean more work. There will be fines, for no matter how closely they guard their reindeer, they cannot control them entirely. "We've no choice but to keep watch over them, if we don't want the

67

Norwegians to slap fines on us." Ándom Ovllá is a leader responsible for his district. He's the man who represents Romssavággi's reindeer herders in any conflicts of interest, a position he has held for only a year or so. He senses the county police officer's critical scrutiny.

"He doesn't grasp that it's me he has to talk to. I'm just a child as far as he's concerned."

In the past, it was generally Ándom Ovllá's father, Juhána Ánte, who negotiated any fines that had to be paid. After his sudden death, this duty fell to his son. Ándom Ovllá finds it hard to speak Norwegian. He listens. But what he says makes little difference anyway; he knows which farmers are favorably inclined, just as he knows which ones will always insist on payment. There are people who don't want them here.

Ándom Ovllá strides up the gully from Goahccevuopmi. The first section, along the mountainside falling away in a sheer drop, is hard going. Once he has reached the plateau, he crosses dried-out mires and alpine meadows at a lope. The peaks on the large islands of Sállir and Ráneš appear to the west, with the open sea beyond. It takes him about half a day to reach home. Though it's not far, the terrain is steep.

His *goahti* stands in Romssavággi on the western side of Stuoranjárga. The growing town of Romsa lies just more than five kilometers away on an offshore island. From time to time the family rows across to the town, or they hop on the milk boat when it passes.

He glimpses wisps of smoke rising from the *goahtis*. From a distance they all look just the same: windowless huts built of peat, with east-facing door openings, strewn across the valley floor like anthills. Straggly tree trunks have been placed against the walls to keep goats from scrambling up. The other end of the valley is overlooked by Šalašoavi, a bow-shaped mountain. In the distance, he can hear dogs barking.

Ándom Ovllá has summered here all his life, often arriving with his herd as early as May. "This is good land: wide open spaces and fine peaks. Grass everywhere. Our calves are well fed and grow big. And we never lose any reindeer around here." He misses his reindeer on the days when he's not out with them.

Stuoranjárga has gradually begun to feel like home to Ristiinná, too. His wife has just hung out the bedclothes to air, throwing stripy, shaggy *rátnus,* sheepskins, reindeer hides, and pillows over the *holga* outside their *goahti.* This is their second summer as a married couple. She and Ándom Ovllá alternate between spending a lot of time together and not seeing each other at all. There are times when he's away more than he's at home in their *goahti.* They had barely met before they married, having grown up on opposite sides of the sea, as Ándom Ovllá puts it. Ristiinná is an Ittohat, a native of Itton-járga. Her summers were spent in the shadow of the Lyngen Alps. In winter, she would ski on one side of Rostu and he on the other. He saw her for the first time at her confirmation in Gárasavvon. She was so much taller and statelier than any other woman there. When she sings her own joik, Ristiinná arches her neck like a crane. "She was so young when I first saw her, but I knew straight away that I wanted to marry her. I knew she was the wife for me."

Although Ándom Ovllá would have preferred to build a larger herd before asking for Ristiinná's hand in marriage, he had to move swiftly. Ristiinná's family were about to be relocated. "She can't stay here if we're not married," he thought. He wound his shoe bands carefully around his best *nuvttahat* and donned the fur with the white edging. A friend spoke on his behalf, while he spent most of the time sitting silently by the door of his future in-laws' *goahti.* His hands were trembling. Everyone knows stories about men who went to ask for a woman's hand in marriage but came home with empty eyes. Ándom Ovllá was afraid that would be his lot. It took a long time for Ristiinná's stepmother to offer him a cup of coffee. She thought he had come too early. "She made it clear: you're not getting any more out of me." She marshaled all the arguments she could find. It was clear she didn't want to lose Ristiinná. Ándom Ovllá was on the verge of going home, but Ristiinná wasn't one to give in so easily. She took him along to the pastor and saw to it that the banns were published.

Ristiinná's family left just a day or so after their wedding. Ándom Ovllá gave them a hand on the first stage of their journey. "Half the people in the district left—including my sister and one of my brothers. Only one stayed on." Ristiinná said farewell to nearly her entire family: her younger brothers, her parents, and her sister, all of whom were packed off to Árjepluovve.

Overnight, Ristiinná became both a new bride and a *stuoranjár-gajohtti.*

Her face was serious when the couple went to have their photograph taken. In the picture, Ristiinná is wearing a cap with a broad band of lace as white as newly fallen snow and a flowered shawl tucked into her *ohca.* Her silver adornments are freshly burnished. The pom-pom on Ándom Ovllá's cap is so large that it hangs forward over his head, making him look slightly taller than he really is. He is smiling contentedly at the photographer.

His father would be pleased, he's sure of that. "*Isá* used to say that my wife should be a believer and not too vain. I took that to heart." Ristiinná would never dream of missing a prayer meeting. It does her good to listen to the pastor's sermon and sing the hymns of Zion. She enjoys the fellowship of the other women when they congregate in the narrow wooden pews.

In mid-August they gather the herd together for the calf slaughtering. They marked the calves a few weeks ago on patches of compacted snow up in the mountains. The young reindeer aren't delicate little creatures anymore; they have grazed and filled out and grown their autumn coats, glossy, velvety, and fine in texture, so soft that your hand feels as if it will melt when you stroke them.

Ristiinná selects the darkest calves. She needs five hides for an adult's garment but fewer to clothe a child. Ristiinná has felt her body changing during the course of the spring. Her breasts have grown larger, and her monthly indisposition has stopped. In some ways she's prepared for motherhood. She has spent her time sewing, baking, laundering, and helping to raise seven younger brothers. In Dillá and Mihkel Biera's family home, they went through large sacks of rye flour each month. There were times when Ristiinná did nothing but put wood on the fire and roll out *gáhkku*. Lying as far inside the *goahti* as they could get, next to the *soggi,* her little brothers would pipe up: "Ristiinná, Ristiinná, give me a piece of bread." Unlike many other girls, she has never worked with reindeer; she's always been needed in the family home.

Ristiinná stretches out the still moist hides on the ground, while Ándom Ovllá deals with the meat. The mournful grunting of the mother reindeer continues until late in the evening. A herd of reindeer bereft of their young will search for them on the spot where the calves went missing. Those who hear them feel their stomachs knot up; no one can become inured to the grief of the mother reindeer.

Ándom Ovllá slaughters almost only calves, just like his father. Juhána Ánte taught Ándom Ovllá everything he knew, and Ándom Ovllá followed him wherever he went. While they wandered over Stuoranjárga, Juhána Ánte would tell him about particular features of the mountains and about the calving grounds. He would show his son special places that he needed to know about, rocks and geological formations in the landscape where people leave gifts and choose their words with care. He told Ándom Ovllá that thanks to Stuoranjárga, their reindeer had the finest antlers to be found anywhere along the coast.

These days, Ándom Ovllá carves his own initials into reindeer horn. He stops at the same places. He honors the land. "I follow my father and honor my parents," he rather solemnly says.

As late summer and early fall meld into the next season, the tourist guide from Romsa comes to announce that the last boat is about to land. Tall North American tourists tramp up the path to the valley. Ándom Ovllá tries to stay in the background when they arrive. To be allowed to continue living in this area, they're obliged to round up the reindeer and put them on show. The worst thing is when the tourists want to touch their clothes, pose in borrowed *gáktis*, or buy the boxes where they keep their valuables or other belongings. They ask them to climb on their *goahtis* and arrange their children in a row. Sometimes they find themselves encircled, hardly able to move, and even so the tourists are often affronted when asked to pay for the photographs they take. The children happily sell pointed letter openers, while the women set out an array of leather pouches. Tourist souvenirs. They make quite a bit of money.

In the days that follow, the herdsmen set out to round up the reindeer. The animals have started to migrate eastward of their own accord, and Ándom Ovllá observes that the older reindeer "know exactly which rocks lie on either side of the trail." There's hardly any need to herd them.

They accompany the herd down to the end of Gáranasvuotna fjord, wait for the ebb tide, and walk along the shoreline for five kilometers. The reindeer nibble at seaweed, and the dogs drive them onward. The air smells of salt water and wet sand.

Ristiinná and the others ride down to the seashore in a horse-drawn cart. They take the steamboat up the fjord, where they meet the herd and lasso the geldings that are to pull the sleds. The *ráidu* takes the same track it used when migrating westward a few months back. The worst part is the journey from the fjord up to the border. There are so many stories about Várreovda, the mountainside overlooking the valley of Čieknjalvuovdi. Puppies have been known to fall into a brook and be swept away. Then there was the woman who stumbled and pulled the pack reindeer with her for some way down the mountainside. Springtime is avalanche season.

They rest only briefly. When the draft reindeer need a rest, they are relieved of their load but left in harness. Ristiinná is quite rotund by now. She sits down on the sleds to rest whenever possible.

On reaching Bikču, Ándom Ovllá pulls the winter provisions out of the *buoggi*. The storage place seems to have survived well enough since they were last here. Then he turns the sleds, stacked upside down on top of one another, the right way up. The lingering scent of the pine tar applied in spring prickles his nose. They load the sleds with the heavy fabric that covers the *goahtis* in winter and the pelts they stored here, with warm, soft shoes and dry provisions. There's a faint whiff of mold from damp fabric, but everything has survived; nothing's been spoiled by mice. They still have dry flour, salt, and coffee. While the *ráidu* moves off slowly toward the east, Ristiinná stays on in Gobmevuohppi. The mantle of snow is almost translucent, barely covering the ground. The Rostu highlands are like a sea, flat and treeless. All that Ristiinná can think of is that she has to go farther east before giving birth. She hires a girl as a companion, and they find a horse-drawn cart to take them to Nearvá.

At the end of November, Ristiinná gives birth to twins at the Eliaksens' farm. Along with physical exhaustion, there's confusion at the discovery that she wasn't carrying just one baby but two. Two little girls. Did she have any inkling of this? The babies arrived earlier than she had calculated, and they feel tiny, birdlike in her arms. They decide to christen them Márge and Elle.

Both Ristiinná and Ándom Ovllá know that the other knows. They can't take two newborn babies with them; two *gietkkamánát* won't survive in their *goahti*. The infants are as fragile as newborn calves, and both have to be fed from Ristiinná's tired body. Winter has barely begun. "*Ii johttiolmmoš sáhte,*" says Ándom Ovllá. Ristiinná was given away by her father as a newborn baby after her mother died in childbirth. She grew up in a foster family and among her mother's siblings. When her father eventually brought her home, she was afraid to enter his *goahti*.

The air feels thin; she can barely breathe. How can they choose which of the two little girls to take with them? She can't ask the crucial question: that task falls to Ándom Ovllá. He has inherited his host family, or *verdde*, the Eliaksens, from his father. Their families have helped each other for as long as he can remember.

"Could one of the girls stay with you?" he asks them in Finnish. That's fine, they reassure him: little Elle can stay with their family. Ándom Ovllá promises to supply them with food, hides, reindeer milk, and whatever else he can. Ándom Ovllá and Ristiinná are well provided for; they have had the weather on their side. The reindeer born last year have had calves, and the winters have been mild, so the Rostu herd has grown. The more important *isidat* like Ándom Ovllá are now slightly better off, while those with smaller herds have gotten back on their feet. He is thankful for his *verdde*'s generosity. "They have so many children of their own, yet they're still ready to look after another one."

Though it breaks her heart to leave her baby daughter behind, Ristiinná has to learn how to take care of the other little one. She lays little Márge in the *gietkka*; Elle will have no need of the cradle with her foster family. When she no longer needs to be suckled and is big enough, they will take both girls on the journey to Stuoranjárga. Ándom Ovllá will fetch Elle as quickly as possible, he promises Ristiinná. He wants to pass on to his children the trails he learned to follow. He will mark calves for them. He wants them to inherit what he was given. The calves to be born in summer will form an inheritance for those coming after him. Everything Juhána Ánte gave him he wants to pass on to his own children.

It doesn't occur to either him or Ristiinná that they, too, may be forced to migrate to a new place and to travel on without one of their daughters. They don't know that little Elle will be left behind, learn Finnish, and forget her mother and father.

"*Eidde* left me in a village with a Swedish woman . . . They traveled on with their *ráidu*, you see, and she couldn't cope with two babies who needed to be suckled. So I stayed behind. She left me with a Swedish woman in the village. First they moved on to the Johkamohki district, and they spent their summers in Váisá.

I was three years old when *isá* came to fetch me. By that time he was like a stranger, my father . . . and my mother . . . I hadn't seen them for several years, you see. And I cried when he came to pick me up by car. I remember that, even though I was so little at the time. The only language I could speak was Finnish, I'd never heard anyone speak Sámi. You cry at that age, of course. I missed my foster mother so badly . . .

In 1931 we had to move here, to Västerbotten, from Váisa. The powers that be sent us here. We started school in that year: it started early, on the first of July. We didn't get to spend any time at home . . . The powers that be sent us here."

Ándom Ovllá Elle
Ella Blind, daughter of Ándom Ovllá and Ristiinná,
forcibly displaced in 1926

75

~~Lappen~~ im Hafen von Tromsö

shmit

Romsavákk ´nieiddat

"They coped well, somehow: whether it was because they were survivors or because they were fearless, I don't know. We joke about it being the survivors who were forced to leave, not the softies." (Laughs)

Did your parents tell you anything about how it was for them?

"My mother was the one who suffered most from home-sickness. But it wasn't something they talked about much. We had no family down here, and when you lose your language as well, who are you supposed to talk to? The language faded away more and more. Every step took them further away. But reindeer were reindeer. They knew they'd survive as long as their reindeer did."

Is Hemavan home to you?

"It's where I grew up . . . so yes, of course it is. Mind you, there's better land up north. If I could choose where to have my *siida*, it'd be in Rostu, no two ways about it. There's so much open land. Reindeer heaven. Good grazing in every tussock . . . When they came down here, they didn't know where the reindeer had got to if they wandered off. The snow was often crusted over with ice, and Nilsá *váidni* used to say that not a single reindeer would have survived if it hadn't been for the beard lichen. I remember them knocking it down with long sticks. No, it's the north that's the land of the reindeer. *Hui!*"

Have you been up to Stuoranjárga, where they used to live?

"Yes, I've traveled around there, been nearly everywhere.

I've been up to Romssavággi with Johánas, but they'd pulled everything down and turned the area beside the brook, where the *goahtis* used to stand, into a shooting range. There's no way you can tell that they once lived there. It's been turned into a playground for other folk . . . It was strange, looking at where they once lived and thinking about how we ended up in Västerbotten. All those people who had to move on to new places . . . And that was all, I suppose . . . No money could have made up for what they lost."

Ándom Ovllá Olle
Olle Omma, son of Ándom Ovllá and Ristiinná,
who were forcibly displaced in 1926

We have a book about our extended family. The pages are coming loose from its binding, and I leaf through it until it comes apart, scribbling notes in the margins. In Johannes Marainen's book *Karesuando sameslätker* (The Sámi Families of Karesuando), forced displacement is superimposed like a grid on many extended families. Nearly all of them saw some of their kin unwillingly displaced.

The women in the book absorb my attention. I count the children they lost. The family book has separate entries for those who did not survive, if the baby's umbilical cord was a tangled *suohpan* or the silver button failed to provide protection. My own *máttáráhkku* Risten lost four children; one died just a year or so before the displacements. So many women were forcibly relocated when they were expecting or their babies were still in their cradles. They were forced to walk across country with heavy bellies.

My own little ones are born while I'm listening to all these stories. The boy who was born in a snowdrift or the little lad they pulled out with the help of a rag soaked in ether and a pothook. The woman who gave birth in a *goahti* in the middle of a forced migration. Thinking of the twins who were separated, I feel the pain in my very backbone. What harm would it have done to my own little three-year-old if I hadn't been able to take her home with me, breathe in her scent, stroke her hair? Who would I have been forced to become to survive that?

The summer of 1925 is to be Ándom Ovllá and Ristiinná's last on Stuoranjárga. In that summer, Sweden's Parliament adopts a

80

new law making it easier for the Lapp Authority to force reindeer herders to relocate or cull their herd. Under this law, forced relocation becomes a legal instrument, meaning that people can now be displaced without any prior investigation. "The Law Concerning the Reduction, in Certain Cases, of the Number of Reindeer within a Lapp Herding Community" is expressly designed to reduce reindeer numbers in various Sámi herding communities. Since there is no longer any need for the reindeer herders to sign letters of application, the authorities can now move them about between Sámi communities more easily, as they see fit. This gives the Lapp Authority a tool that it lacked in the past.

Ándom Ovllá and Ristiinná prefer to relocate rather than cull their herd: you want your reindeer to live so that you too can live.

Certain words crop up again and again in documents and quotations from this period. Incapable. Disorderly. Primitive. A people in need of assistance, for their own good. The forced resettlements take place at a time when Sweden is bent on organizing the lives of those deemed unable to do it themselves. There are new regulations prohibiting Sámi people from moving into houses or modernizing their *goahtis* too much. Allow them too much comfort, and they might be tempted to abandon their nomadic way of life. There are bans on speaking their own language. Nomad schools. Assimilation. The harsh policies of the early twentieth century include coercion of various kinds, ranging from forced displacement to the slaughter of reindeer.

This is the era of "racial biology" research. Measuring naked people. Excavating graves in search of skulls and skeletons.

All of this goes hand in hand with stronger powers for the Lapp Authority. According to history professor Patrik Lantto, the Lapp Authority controlled much of a Sámi reindeer herder's life in the 1920s. The Lapp bailiffs ration strong drink and flour, and they determine reindeer numbers. The Lapp bailiffs also decide where individual families are to be moved in the context of the forced relocations.

The new law is adopted in 1925 because of the reindeer glut at that time. Twenty thousand animals are to be moved out of Sweden's northernmost Sámi herding communities. More families have to leave now. This time they have to be sent farther afield, as Norrbotten county is full. The districts of Jåhkåmåkke (Jokkmokk), Jiellevárre (Gällivare), and Árjepluovve (Arjeplog) have already taken in more than two hundred people and their reindeer herds over four years. There's no room for any more. The authorities now have the counties of Västerbotten and Jämtland in their sights.

SVENSK FÖRFATTNINGSSAMLING.

1925
Nr 181—183.

Utkom från trycket
den 18 juni 1925.

Nr 181.

Lag

angående minskning i vissa fall av renantalet inom lappby;

given Stockholms slott den 6 juni 1925.

(Rubrik och datum kungöras från predikstolen.)

Vi GUSTAF, med Guds nåde, Sveriges, Götes och Vendes Konung, göra veterligt: att Vi, med riksdagen[1], funnit gott att, med upphävande av 8 § i lagen den 1 juli 1898 (nr 66) om de svenska lapparnes rätt till renbete i Sverige, förordna som följer:

1 §.

1. Därest inom lappby antalet renar befinnes vara så stort, att betesmarkerna måste anses otillräckliga eller att genom renarna betydande skadegörelser förorsakas, och inom lappbyn finnas renar, tillhörande andra än lappar, må länsstyrelsen, efter det lapparna blivit hörda, förordna, att så stort antal av dessa renar, som prövas för ändamålet nödigt, inom viss förelagd tid skall från lappbyn avlägsnas, vid äventyr att renarna av lappbyns ordningsman omhändertagas och levande eller slaktade för ägarnas räkning försäljas. Närmare föreskrifter i fråga om verkställighet härav meddelas av länsstyrelsen, som darvid har att tillse såväl att de särskilda renägarnas rätt och bästa i görligaste mån bevaras som ock att rensk ande lapp icke i oskälig grad kringskäres i sin näring.

2. Befinnes, sedan med tillämpning av 1 mom. renar, tillhörande andra än lappar, avlägsnats från lappby, de återstående renarnas antal ändock vara för stort, äge länsstyrelsen, efter det lapparna såväl i nämnda lappby som i lappby, dit inflyttning kan ifrågakomma, blivit hörda, hänvisa en eller flera lappar till annan lappby, där utrymme finnes och dit inflyttning utan avsevärd olägenhet kan ske. Härvid skall länsstyrelsen tillse, att lapp, som själv eller vars förfäder länge tillhört lappbyn eller inom dess område haft rätt till bete för sina renar, icke utan synnerliga skäl mot sin vilja hänvisas till annan lappby.

Hänvisas lapp att med de renar, som äro under hans vård, flytta till annan lappby, förelägge länsstyrelsen honom vid vite att inom viss tid hava verkställt flyttningen samt meddele honom i övrigt de föreskrifter, som med av-

Should the Lapp, with the reindeer under his care, be instructed to relocate to another Lapp herding community, the County Administrative Board must inform him that he must have completed his move within a given period of time and must also inform him of the regulations by which he must abide in so doing. Should the Lapp fail to carry out the relocation within the prescribed period of time, the County Administrative Board shall either impose further fines and/or order the reindeer to be transferred and taken care of at the expense of the refractory party.

FROM "THE LAW CONCERNING THE REDUCTION, IN CERTAIN CASES, OF THE NUMBER OF REINDEER WITHIN A LAPP HERDING COMMUNITY," 1925

De dolin de juo
Dolin de juo
Dolin de juo dolin de

Biera mága luodi juo
de juoiggastit de juoiggastit

De Biera máhka
dolin dolin
de vuodjelii

3,000 duhát ealu
Biera máhka
čuoiggadii

De oarjjásguvlui
Biera máhka
láidestii

Rostuvuomi
dáčča skuovaid
fuomašii

Way back when
Way back when
Way back when, way back

Brother-in-law Biera's yoik
they yoiked and yoiked

Brother-in-law Biera
back then, back then
He used to drive the herd forward

a reindeer herd of 3000 head
Brother-in-law Biera
he used to ski beside

to southern tracts
Brother-in-law Biera
brought the herd to rest

At Rostuvuomi
Norwegian shoes
he noticed

Duhpaha čolggai
Bieara máhka
čolggadii

De duolluid dálluid
maŋosguvlui
vilppastii

De garraseappot
ovddosguvlui
huškkodii
fáškkudii

De garraseappot ovddosguvlui
Biera máhka čuoiggadii

Tobacco he spit
Brother-in-law Biera
he used to spit

Now and again
to similar places
he turned his glance

the harder
forward
he pressed
he strove

The harder the going forward
Brother-in-law Biera skied

Biera máhka
Brother-in-law Biera's joik

ubmeje tjeïlddie

7

Ná dat lea ipmil gohččun neavrri dahkat
God Gave This Job to the Devil Himself

AUGUST 1925

Biito Biera

Biito Biera and his hired hand rise early to finish the fishing. Biito Biera has a dim recollection of his dream, which was about Ánne. He tries to shake it off. They hang the cotton fishing net out to dry and make a fire of willow twigs. The hired man takes the fish fat and pours it into a dish. Although it's the same routine each morning, Biito Biera freezes now when he sees the grease congeal: it formed a misshapen but well-defined cross. He grabs the dish.

"We've got to finish here and get going."

"Right now? But we need to eat first."

The hired man protests, but Biito Biera steps out of the *goahti* and pulls the cover off, leaving the poles exposed. It's a small *čogogoahti* and doesn't take long to dismantle. The hired man has no choice but to pack. The net is already hanging over the *buoggi*, their only storage place. Flour, salt, and coffee: they tie everything that's left to the *buoggi*. Working together, they heave the *goahti* cover over their belongings and lash it down. Biito Biera is usually painstaking about his work, but this time things will have to do as they are. He usually says a few words to protect whatever they leave behind, but there's no time for that now. Although he can't recall the details of his dream, the feeling it left grows within him.

It's nearly twenty kilometers from Rostujávri to Gorvvejávri.

The hillsides are carpeted in an intractable tangle of sallow bushes. Biito Biera takes long strides, too long. He stumbles. Further up the mountainside they can increase their pace.

By the time they near Gorvvejávri that afternoon, Mihkela Máret has already spotted them. Biito Biera's mother is stronger than you'd think. She rows across the lake with powerful strokes, the sleeves of her *gákti* partly rolled up, her back toward them in the stubby wooden skiff. The smoke rises from the *goahtis* on the other side of the lake. She gives them a nod.

"What's happened?"

"Things could be better," she replies. She remains silent a little too long. "It's not gone the way it should have. Ánne's sick. She's been ill this past day and night."

Mihkela Máret tells him they have sent for Marie Steen, the *čalbmeeadni*, but it's nearly a hundred kilometers to Målselv. Each hour they spend waiting for the midwife feels as long as a famine year.

When Marie Steen finally comes pattering toward them, they usher her straight into the *goahti*. After a long time, she emerges, shaking her head.

"It's impossible, the baby's stuck. We've got to get the doctor here."

Biito Biera starts to run, taking nothing with him. The nearest telephone belongs to the Stenvolds, who live at the first farm near Frihetsli, fifty kilometers away. His *gákti* is soaked in sweat by the time he arrives. Someone has to ring the doctor, he yells.

He wanders around for several hours. His memories are both misty and as clear as ice. Why did he listen to Ánne when she insisted on staying up in the mountains? Others had coped, she'd said, and she was no less capable than they. She trusted Rihttamuore to deliver the baby. His Ánne, his Jovnesa Ánne. He ought to have put his foot down.

He had seen the signs, after all, like when the pack reindeer suddenly took to their heels after his journey to ask for Ánne's hand in marriage. They had raced off with their tongues hanging out, leaving only a cloud of snow behind them. Or when they were getting married and his legs gave way . . . There was so much he hadn't understood, although he had seen it himself. Ánne had worn a new silken shawl to church: he can see it so clearly in his mind's eye.

The doctor arrives on horseback behind Biito Biera, who leads the way on foot. They wade across the broad stream a few kilometers above Frihetsli. That's as far as they get. Marie Steen is approaching from the southern side. She's on her way home.

"She didn't make it . . . nor did the baby; it was stuck," says Marie Steen. Biito Biera sits down on the bank.

He has no sense of how long he stays there. He starts looking for pebbles in the brook. He weighs them in his hand, cold and wet, and starts building a small cairn beside the path. Using his long knife to whittle a cross, he writes on the fresh, damp wood that it was here the news arrived: "Anna Blind has died." He and Ánne had been given one year together as a married couple.

At the camp, an upended log holds the *goahti* door open. Carefully, they lift Ánne out and lay her beside the *goahti*, using part of its cover to wrap her body. In the lake there is an island that cannot be reached by animals. They lay Ánne in a boat-shaped sled and row her over. This will be her summer grave, where she can lie until the snow comes.

Biito Biera's father had recommended Ánne. "Go and talk to Jovnes *áddjá*; he has a fine granddaughter." Biito Biera saddled two reindeer geldings, one for himself and the other for the friend who promised to speak on his behalf. "We traveled from Láttevárri and then three or four kilometers south from Silkemuotki. When I arrived they were all so good-humored . . . I spent three days there with the Jovnesa *siida*. There was no need to hurry on anywhere else, and the pasture was good . . ." Ánne and he went to the church without delay to tell the pastor about their plans.

Everything went so quickly. Shortly after the wedding they became better off, and Ánne's belly grew. They planned to build their reindeer herd together.

"I can't grasp what's happened. I work all day and weep at night." He can't take it in, that the tent he sleeps in is empty.

The mountains around them soon fill with other families traveling east from the summering grounds on the coast. All these family groups are on their way to their winter grazing lands. The nights are clear and starry. Biito Biera feels his back grow ever colder; when he lies down to sleep, the fire warms only the front of his body. Once the fire dies, his *goahti* is as cold as ice. The snow turns the highest peaks white first, then creeps farther and farther down the mountainside. Soon the ground is moist and white.

Before the ice forms on the lake, they bring Ánne's *geres* home. The sled in which she lies, bedded on brushwood, is drawn by one of her own reindeer. The white pennant tied to its antlers flutters in the wind. They bring Ánne to the church mortuary.

During the Christmas feast days, one *ráidu* after another glides into Gárasavvon along the frozen river. The people wear their best furs and shoes of reindeer hide, white as the hoarfrost on the trees. During religious feast days the church square fills with *ráidus*. People come to purchase supplies, court, christen their children, bury their dead, and marry. They come to pick the fleetest draft reindeer and to meet friends they wouldn't otherwise see. The church, standing on a ridge that slopes steeply down to the river, keeps watch over the village. Sleds lie scattered here and there outside the hotel, as the villagers call the old courthouse behind the church. Those who don't stay there go to their usual host family, their *verdde*. Those without a host family put up their *goahti* on the outskirts of the village.

90

Usually Biito Biera strolls around among the *goahtis*, but this time the only people he meets are the ones who drop by. They chat about pasture and predators, about those who have passed on and those who have just come into the world. Many discuss the authorities' new law. They say your reindeer herd will be culled or confiscated if you refuse resettlement. There are rumors that the *sivnnar,* Lapp Inspector Lidström, is traveling around with his book. "Some people are being forced to move—to the Dearna district, even as far away as Vilhelmina. They hand us a pen and tell us where to sign."

Máhte Heaikka refuses. He won't leave Stuoranjárga. Others have asked for permission to move down to kinfolk in Jåhkåmåkke. No one wants to go to Västerbotten. Has anyone been there, *duon riikas,* in that country?

On the second day of Christmas, 1925, Anni Maria Bals (Jovnesa Ánne) is buried. The sky is overcast and it has stopped snowing. The church pews are full. Some of the women sit on the floor holding cradles. Young children whimper and people comfort them. Shrill voices sing hymns in Finnish. Prayers. Outside the church, Ánne's relatives break into a joik of mourning, a monotonous sound between ululation and weeping. First they kneel beside her sled, then at her grave.

Over Christmas, Biito Biera meets Ristiinná, the daughter of his mother's brother Mihkel Biera. All his cousins are like siblings to him, and she's no exception. The Lapp bailiff has given Ristiinná and Ándom Ovllá an ultimatum: "Slaughter or start on your journey."

"Take me with you," Biito Biera says to Ándom Ovllá. "Nothing's going well here anyway. I have nothing left." He pictures the journey southward. Compensation. Hired men. A relocation allowance. The idea has taken root within him. "Soon my parents-in-law are going to cull my two hundred reindeer, leaving only two. That's if they want to, but I'm guessing that they will."

He's not about to cull his reindeer and start again from scratch, Ándom Ovllá says. He's only just built up his herd. So the decision is made: they will travel south together.

Throughout January, Biito Biera keeps the reindeer to the west of the horse track that runs past Mount Guorpmek, linking Sohppar and Gárasavvon. Mihkela Máret sits by the fireside, pulling glowing splinters out of the embers. She sucks the glow into her pipe, lighting it. She's as tough as a birch tree, his mother, and becoming more wiry with each year that passes. When the family lost all their reindeer in the *goavvi* that saw half the Rostu herd starve to death, they began fishing in Lake Rostujávri and hunting Arctic foxes. In springtime, his father would fashion sleds for passing travelers, two each spring. Mihkela Máret sold pelts and shoes. Each year she'd knot two new fishing nets, though she still talked about the reindeer herd they'd once had; for her, fishing was a mere stopgap. No star shone brighter than Mihkela Máret when Biito Biera got on his feet again and started to build up a herd through barter. She'd tuck a piece of bread into the *ohca* of his *gákti* when he was on his way out. He's always been her little boy.

Now she's loaded up her sleds with goods from the north. Bags, handmade items, shoe bands, and ladles. She hasn't left as much as a needle behind.

Ándom Ovllá and Ristiinná arrive in February. Biito Biera lets his reindeer mingle with theirs. "We had several *ráidus*: my mother led one, and my hired hand another. We must have had well over a thousand reindeer. When we reached Giron, Nils Omma caught up with us. With the two brothers, that made at least two thousand. I can't recall the exact number."

Their documents say they have been assigned to the Sámi herding community of Umbyn, but Ándom Ovllá and Biito Biera hope to stay in the mountains of Jåhkåmåhkke. Both Biito Biera and Ristiinná want to be near their extended family. Who knows, maybe they can stay there? They have heard of others who have done the same or who plan to. The powers that be make the occasional exception. So folk say.

Biito Biera looks around. Whenever he thinks of Ánne, the grief nearly kills him. Every rock and boulder around Sohppar reminds him of her.

"It's the devil that's throwing me out," he claims. "God gave this job to the devil himself."

"After all these years, I've been wondering whether they sang so much because of the people they missed. They'd talk about the time when they lived in Mielli, and about the big gatherings there . . . There were big prayer meetings. At Christmas, there'd always be lots of people coming to Gárasavvon for the Christmas Mass. And then they had to come down here . . . to this place. People never gather together here. There's nowhere to go. So people were scattered hither and thither, and they used to say, 'Like lost sheep, we were, some of us here, some of us there.' And then they'd remember the songs they'd learned up north . . ."

Báluha Biette Biret Márjá
Brita-Maria Utsi, forcibly displaced in 1923

"We came to Skielldavárre as strangers. We stopped in Sarddá. Then some people arrived, *oarjelat*. Dáve *áddjá* said, 'Here come some Swedes with lassoes over their shoulders,' and I called out to him, 'They're Sámi! They have a *ráidu* of pack reindeer.' Then we moved on to Bieskehávrre, near Sulitelma, and when the fall came their reindeer mingled with ours.

We built a corral by the shores of Bieskehávrre. A brushwood corral. My father built it together with the Báluhat and Lánggut families and Giertto Biette. And the *oarjelat* began withdrawing their reindeer from the herd. They'd never seen a reindeer corral before and thought it was strange that we used them: that wasn't the way they did things. They didn't really approve of our corrals. You're making the animals suffer, they said. They could do without, you see, their reindeer were so docile . . . Tame as goats, they were. They used small sleds on their migrations, *gierresat* that looked like toys . . . They were amazed that the Karesuando people had such big draft reindeer. Their own animals were small and as black as soot. But now their reindeer have interbred with ours. And the people have influenced each other too. Nowadays they build corrals and they've become real *suohpangiehta*, skilled at lassoing reindeer. We've taught them all kinds of tricks.

And they were good herdsman, *hirbma!* They never lost a reindeer herd in the meadows; the reindeer would never run off, they were so tame. And they had big herds.

We had a man responsible for law and order, Nils Ánte Grufvisare. A tough *ortnet*, he was. He was so angry, he cursed the *nuorttut* for building corrals. Tormenting the reindeer! He grabbed Ovllá Ándaras by the beard and led him out of the corral. *Dån la mujsta miesev ädjám. Ädjám* was what they'd say in a case of false marking. He thought Ovllá Ándaras had marked their calves, but he'd only marked the odd one or two."

Guhmusa Heaika
Henrik Nilsson Kuhmunen,
forcibly relocated to Árjepluovve in 1923

I cross another person's name off my list of interviewees. We had been talking about meeting, but it didn't work out, and later he became too frail. I spotted his obituary with the reindeer at the top, as is the tradition with reindeer herders. Now I'm scrapping all the questions I'd written down. I don't know anyone else who knows the things he did.

Instead, I look for belongings people took with them on their journeys to new country. I find a faded belt. A flowered cloth bag gathered with a woven band. A pair of worn-out shoes inherited and worn by one of the children. Some took with them the papers issued by the Lapp Authority, the decisions they had feared. Crumpled typewritten documents couched in convoluted Swedish. Where did they keep these papers? In a *giisá*, among their silver items and other valuables? Could they even read them?

Sweden, too, has kept items for posterity. Behind blank, stone-framed windows, the archive in Härnösand that houses the Lapp Authority's documents contains shelf after shelf of papers sorted into unbleached cardboard folders. In the chilly research room, I leaf through papers wearing white cotton gloves. Some letters plead; others protest. Though many of the signatories needed help with their letters, some members of Sámi herding communities, such as Anta Pirak and Gustav Park, had learned how to advocate for their community. The voices of the displaced people are largely absent from the archive materials, but there are letters from Sámi communities farther south, where some people learned the authorities' language. They protest against being forced to accept more reindeer on their grazing lands.

In 1926, meetings are held with Sámi herding communities in Västerbotten county. They say no to more reindeer and to an influx of reindeer from farther north. They need the pastureland for their own reindeer. Yet the Lapp Authority continues undeterred. Protests and discontent surface in the journal *Samefolket* (The Sámi People) and elsewhere. Herders from the herding communities farther south protest in readers' letters. Why is the Lapp Authority ignoring their views? Reindeer husbandry differs between regions. The communities farther south have smaller herds that they watch over more intensively. They feel their herds are being swamped by those coming from the north.

These conflicts spread, becoming toxic, yet the Lapp Authority continues to assure those concerned that everything will get better. The new arrivals will adjust soon enough. The Lapp bailiffs allocate the forcibly displaced people to different locations: one family here, another there, each *siida* assigned its own area. If larger settlements are forcibly split up, the displaced people will probably adapt more easily to keeping smaller herds, so the thinking goes.

The new arrivals are trying to achieve the opposite: moving discreetly toward each other, "creeping closer," as they put it. If objections are raised, they can often come up with a reasonable justification: the condition of the snow and ice made it impossible to travel onward. These delaying tactics go hand in hand with apologies. The elders are fond of talking about this, a tiny spark of protest in the midst of submission. Humor is like a *beaska*, a pelt you wrap around yourself to ward off a chill draft.

Above all, those who have been ordered to leave for Västerbotten do what they can to put off the journey. All the families concerned try to stay in Norrbotten, and when forced to leave they stop with relatives along the route. When the Lapp bailiffs tell them they can't stay, they have an entire store of pretexts to draw on. No one wants to be the only relocated family in a new Sámi herding community. Extended family roots you to the land, providing links that support and sustain you. Family provides the only connection these people still have.

"It is in your own best interests for you to commence the journey toward your new domicile of your own volition, thereby avoiding any need for coercive measures. The County Administrative Board is not entirely convinced that your lengthy peregrinations here and there, from one Lapp herding community to another, have been strictly necessary. In fact, the Board suspects that your aim in so doing has been to enable you to remain in the Jokkmokk area." This was how Lapp Bailiff Holm, for example, responded to one request.

It soon becomes clear that once the Lapp Authority is resolved to displace a family, displacement is unavoidable. The new law on the reduction of reindeer numbers enables the Lapp Authority to fine anyone who remains "refractory." For reindeer herders whose wealth lies in their herd, not in money, the price is too high. The valuables they may have tucked away in a *giisá* are not enough to purchase their freedom.

Pursuant to Section 2 of the Law of 6 June 1925 concerning the reduction, in certain cases, of the number of reindeer within a Lapp herding community, the County Administrative Board hereby orders you to leave the Lapp herding community of Lainiovuoma together with your reindeer. The relocation is to commence by the end of March 1926, on pain of a fine of 200 kronor. Until such time as another domicile can be made available for you, you are instructed to relocate to the Lapp herding community of Arjeploug . . . Luleå, County Secretariat, 3rd of March 1926.

ON BEHALF OF THE COUNTY
ADMINISTRATIVE BOARD
R. SUNDBY   A. HOLM

"I have been left with only eight draft reindeer, with which I hope to reach my summering grounds, with some help from friendly neighbors. But it is quite a different matter to travel all the way to Arjeplog. For that I would need at least fourteen draft reindeer. If I had known this when I was ordered to reduce the size of my herd, I would have been able to train the reindeer that have now been slaughtered and eaten, so I would have had them as draft animals.

My wife is so weak that she may lose what remains of her sanity if she is forced to move to new country against her will. At this stage in the year, this will ruin us completely, and she will have a breakdown and possibly need hospitalization.

The severe storms that have hit this region have compacted the snow so badly that many of the weaker reindeer are bound to perish on such a journey. In view of the above, I hope that you, in your capacity as County Governor, will understand that I am in a very difficult predicament. It is impossible to find anyone to help us on this migration, and if, contrary to all expectations, any such person or persons were to appear at the last moment, many of the reindeer in my small herd would die along the way anyway, and I would arrive at my destination a ruined man. If I do not move to a new location, but instead

try to stay here with my reindeer until next year, I shall
be fined 200 kronor; in other words, I shall be ruined in
any case. I therefore respectfully appeal to you, as County
Governor, to take pity on me and authorize me to spend
next summer beyond the fence in Saarivuoma: between
Korvijärvi, Juulusjoki, and Soitjutangi, to be precise,
where there have been no reindeer for the past few years,
or, alternatively, farther north, next to Dödesfjäll [Death
Mountain]."

Lannavaara, 11 March 1926
Per Gustafsson Idivuoma
Övre Soppero

The County Administrative Board would also remind you that you were already warned by the Lapp bailiff in November 1925 that you were among the people for whom relocation was deemed appropriate and who were therefore required to submit an application for such relocation. There would have been no need to raise the objections you have brought up concerning difficulties in obtaining help with the journey and a shortage of draft reindeer—objections whose basis in reality the County Administrative Board is unable to judge—had you prepared for your relocation in a timely fashion . . . You should therefore resign yourself to the inevitability of a move to Västerbotten.

G. MALM, COUNTY GOVERNOR, MAY 1926

In cases where a Lapp is "ordered" to leave his home region for a distant destination, there are always grounds of a purely human nature not to enforce such relocation in accordance with the regulations. However, if one were to relent for such reasons, it would be impossible to maintain order, either in this case or in others.

LETTER FROM LAPP BAILIFF HOLM, 1927

Grer kanis

Ristena Márjá

8

Hearráváldi
Subjugation

APRIL 1928

Márjá ja Gusttu Bierar

Anna Maria Idivuoma and Per Gustafsson Idivuoma

Márjá spots her mother walking toward her. Risten is dressed in
hide, with a close-fitting lace-trimmed cap tied under her chin. She
seems to have filled out a little since the last time they met. Her
liidni is wound tightly around her neck. Risten must have heard
the news that her daughter was on her way. They haven't seen each
other since they were forced to leave their homes, not even at Márjá
and Gusttu Bierar's wedding. Risten nods to her daughter.

"I'll lead this one," she says, taking the gelding's reins.

Márjá follows her.

The *goahtis* stand on a heath covered in conifers. A wisp of smoke
rises from the *reahpen* at the top of each *goahti*. The sleds have not
been unloaded, which suggests they will be on their way again soon.
Dogs bark and children play: the sounds of home, though home is
far away now. The lower half of Risten's *goahti* is covered in lengths
of striped woolen cloth, and the upper half in coarse linen, sooty
and patched and mended with long stitches here and there where
the fabric has torn. Snow has been shoveled into heaps around
the dwelling. The firs, slender and coated in frost, grow so close
together that you could sleep out beneath them and not get wet
even if the heavens were to open. The dense forest is punctuated

105

by snow-covered mires. Risten helps Márjá to unbridle and tether the geldings. Márjá's shoulders relax when she spots her brother and sister: quick, wiry Joná, who has shot up like a beanstalk, and Márge, with her smile.

Their neighbor from Láttevárri, who helped them with the *ráidu*, prepares to retrace her steps. She offered to accompany Gusttu Bierar and Márjá when she heard that they would have to leave. Márjá has felt grateful to her for that; the sleds are heavy. It has sometimes felt as if the invisible ones are against the journey. She thanks her neighbor. The response is a brief "Now, now, lass." Maybe they will meet again.

Gusttu Bierar and Márjá make an odd couple. Gusttu Bierar is a head taller than most. He takes long strides, and his features are rough-hewn. Some call him "the giant from Idivuoma." Márjá is the size of a schoolchild and only reaches up as far as her husband's chest. At a distance, you might well take her for his daughter. She tends to smile with her eyes, with a cautious warmth, keeping her mouth closed. A quiet one, many say. Gusttu Bierar greets people and chats with them, and he's learned several languages—as well as Sámi, Finnish, and Norwegian, he even speaks a little Swedish. He gets to know people quickly wherever he goes.

The *goahti* fills with people eager for news from the north. How have the winters been? The grazing? What areas have they traveled through? Gusttu Bierar has stories to tell. Nothing has been the same since the convention took effect. He and Márjá have been fined by both Swedish and Norwegian authorities. They incurred fines in Sweden for refusing to travel south and in Norway for crossing the border. "Two hundred kronor on the Swedish side, and the same on the Norwegian side," says Gusttu Bierar. Even ten kronor is a lot of cash. Now the Lapp Authority is sending them to Västerbotten, but no one knows exactly where they are meant to go. "To the ends of

Gustn Biens

the earth. What do we know about the country or its people or how our reindeer will do there?" But Gusttu Bierar takes the opportunity to boast about his wife. "We have a long *ráidu*, with fourteen sleds. It's hard work for her and no breaks. She may be small, but strength isn't always a matter of size."

The brushwood inside the *goahti* feels soft after those long days spent traveling with the *ráidu*. The bedclothes lie rolled up against the *soggi*. It takes Márjá a while to get used to seeing her brother and sister again. Márge, the sister she took care of from the cradle, is already helping with the cooking. Kneeling, she melts snow and adds salt to the coffee pot. Their mother serves the meal. Risten keeps her changing moods under wraps. As Márjá has learned, her moods can resemble the lands where they spend their summers: the peaks are higher than anywhere else, while the valleys go all the way down to the sea. But she seems to have recovered her spirits, at least partly. The winter pasturage seems to have been better here, too. Her kin have helped her. Márjá's family lost nearly everything they had during the hard years a decade ago, and her *isá* died at the same time. Then came the forced relocations to cap it all off. Risten arranged for Márjá's younger sister Elle to stay with relatives in Gáranasvuotna. As for Márjá, she got married. Márjá often thinks of the quiet sister she loves, Elle with the strong, cold fingers, the girl who launders and milks like no other. Someone told them she has to live in a barn with the cattle. They hope that's just hearsay.

They leave the sleds loaded, unpacking only what they need. The people are on the verge of leaving. Any day now, all the family groups will be setting off westward toward their calving grounds. Early one morning Márjá lashes the hides down and loads the sled with sacks. Dried meat, bread, and coffee she's roasted and ground. They set off early over the ice-encrusted snow. The light is dim.

The weather is fickle. The land has yet to decide whether it's winter or spring. Over to the west, beyond Suorvvá, the sky turns

milk-white and a fuzzy halo forms around the sun. Gusttu Bierar takes the shovel out of the *goahtegeres* to dig holes for the *goahti* poles. They climb to lay the tent fabric over the poles, pull it taut from the inside, and make sure they have firewood and snow to melt into water.

At night the wind rises, making the tent fabric belly and slap. Snow creeps in through the tiniest gap. By the time the blizzard has abated, the cloth is glazed with a fine coating of ice. The wind has traced frozen wave patterns in the snow, covering their tracks. Gusttu Bierar hurries off to tend to the reindeer. He was obliged to slaughter some of the herd before their forced relocation. Only the very best remain, most of them females. There were barely enough left to pull the *ráidu*. Walking about among the reindeer, he feels the panic rising. They're not there. His and Márjá's animals have disappeared. They must have turned northward during the storm; they have headed back toward the north. The others grasp this, too. "I'll go with you," says Ándom Ovllá.

The snow that fell in the blizzard reveals fresh tracks, but it's also given the reindeer a head start. Ándom Ovllá races off with Gusttu Bierar just behind him. Though he's not as fast as he is strong, Gusttu Bierar keeps up the pace. He pulls his cap back off his forehead. Sweat is trickling down his temples. By the time they reach Dievssajávri they have caught up with forty or so reindeer with the right sort of ear marking.

"You round these up," he says to Ándom Ovllá, "and I'll carry on searching."

The hoofprints continue northward toward Mount Giebnegáisi, becoming increasingly indistinct. Other tracks appear, pass by, and intermingle with those of their animals. After skiing for a few more kilometers, Gusttu Bierar comes to a standstill. "Once we're north of Giebnegáisi, I'm stopping. There's nothing but a jumble of different tracks."

Ándom Ovllá recalls the moment when he sees Gusttu Bierar return alone, without any reindeer. "Two days without food, that's hard, but seeing Idivuoma return empty-handed is worse."

When Gusttu Bierar and Márjá set off on their trek south, they had nearly two hundred reindeer. Now barely one hundred remain. More than half the herd has gone. The cows that are due to calve have turned back. They'll never find all the animals they have lost. Now they stand empty-handed on unknown soil. "We've become paupers," says Gusttu Bierar to Márjá. He's wrestling with a new sense of bitterness toward the *hode*, the *sundi*, the *sivnnar*, the *leanska*, call them what you will. These officials exercise different types of power, but make no mistake: the people who mark reindeer are at the bottom of the pecking order.

When the Lapp Authority told them a few years back that they must either accept relocation or slaughter part of their herd, Gusttu Bierar slaughtered some of their animals. He thought that would help, yet he and Márjá were selected for relocation anyway. They asked August Lundberg from Láttevárri for help, and he took down a letter for them. Gusttu Bierar argued his case. He refused to give up. He wasn't about to move. The Lapp bailiff imposed fines, and then more fines. Gusttu Bierar and Márjá had no spare cash, and they couldn't slaughter any more of their herd. How were they to travel without geldings to pull the sleds? What were they supposed to live on? Márjá recalls the moment when she understood that he had given up, when she grasped that they had to leave.

When people hear what's befallen them, they tell them about others who have lost their property. Gusttu Bierar writes to the Lapp bailiff again. Can they auction off or slaughter their reindeer, if they can be found? Can they ask people from other herding communities who know their ear markings to help them?

In summer they set up their *goahti* in a birch forest in Vájsáluo-kta, the new summering grounds for forcibly displaced Sámi. Márjá and Gusttu Bierar's *bealljegoahti* is the only one in the forest. Three *goahtis* belonging to a nomad school for Sámi children, with a Swedish flag fluttering from a pole, stand nearby. The others, built of peat, belong to families from the north. They have built new homes and started to make paths between them. Márjá can't answer when she's asked where they're heading. She doesn't know. The powers that be haven't yet decided. All they know is that they are bound for Västerbotten county.

When travelers pass through, Gusttu Bierar increasingly talks to them about power. "I wish some politician would defend the rights of the oppressed." He raises the issue with clergymen and ethnologists. Sometimes he sounds like a preacher. "It's the border that's done all this damage, that's what's torn our lands apart."

Gusttu Bierar's siblings still live in the north; they were never forced to relocate. His sister has said she'll pay if he wants to come and visit them. "But I dare not go back. Ever. I'm too afraid that if I return I'll never be able to leave again."

"They wept. That's what *eidde* told me. They said farewell to the places where their *goahtis* had stood, and to the poles that had supported them, the Lord help us. They should have got some sort of compensation, that's what I think. The mountains up there are so flat, and here they're so ugly. I've heard there are such lovely flowers up on Bealčán, in the north. My aunt on Mam's side used to cry when she thought of Bealčán. So fond of flowers, she was. They said farewell to them, too. There was a kind of kiosk with a window. They'd stand on either side and weep.

They said a Lapp should stay a Lapp, you know. It was the bailiffs who decided everything, the Lord help us. They were so afraid of those bailiffs. *Isá* was ordered not to leave Guvtjávrre, but he traveled on to Vájsá anyway. They sneaked down there like outlaws.

They were supposed to live in dark *goahtis* without windows. 'Build us a big goahti,' *eidde* said to *isá*, and he did: a *goahti* with windows, up on a hill. It was so full of light, that *goahti*. And *eidde* ordered a stove so she could bake bread. Then along they came, the Lapp bailiff and the district police superintendent, or whoever it was, and told them Lapps had to live in dark homes. No question of having windows. They were ordered to remove them. Then *eidde* was told to pay a fine for having a stove in her home, and for the windows. You lay a finger on my stove and I'll report you, said *eidde*. Touch one nail in this *goahti*, and I'll report you. She wasn't afraid of anyone. But they were terrible, those Lapp bailiffs.

Just put that in your book, will you? Our story. It's all true."

Váikko Elle Susá
Elle Susanna Nordqvist

113

Válkko bhodni,
biette sraitá

"I remember my Gran, Dad's mother, as a born coper. Her husband died when our Dad was ten. And there she was, with five children. When they were deported, if that's the word, she arranged for Elle to stay behind in Norway as a farm maid. It seems terribly hard-hearted of her to have left the youngster behind . . . as if she had no conscience. Because Elle wasn't treated well on that farm. She had to sleep in the barn with the cattle. But Gran must have thought: 'What am I to do?' She was a woman on her own, with a clutch of kids. She had to find some way to cope, I guess. The family lived in *goahtis* (tents) to begin with, and then Gran went back up to fetch Elle. Anyone they didn't have room for here had to keep on going, farther south. The state decided where they were to live and where there was enough room for them. But how in heaven's name did Gran manage to go all the way from Porjus to Tromsø to bring Elle back? I've no idea . . .

It was fun teasing her when we were kids, because it was so easy to get a rise out of her! We'd sit on the roof while she clambered up the ladder. Then we'd jump down from the other side and pull the ladder away. Dad wasn't always around to keep an eye on us, you see, he'd be up in the mountains. But we didn't dare do that kind of thing when he was home.

And she had a temper on her. Dementia, it was. She was pretty confused in her last few summers, it was awful really . . . She'd start jabbering away when the rest of us wanted to go to sleep. And on top of that she was one of those people who could see and hear things others can't. She could see lights before they had electricity in Rijtjem, and when we moved here she could hear church bells before there were any.

I remember they decided to put her in an old people's home when we moved away. She didn't live long after that. Not long, maybe just another month after they'd taken her to the home. Old Sámi people like her died of boredom in old people's homes, I reckon.
What was she like? [*Thinks for a while.*] She was made of stern stuff. Life had made her that way, I guess."

Kristina Lansgren's memories of her paternal grandmother, Risten, who was forcibly displaced in 1923

Three years, say the elders, that's how long it takes for reindeer to get accustomed to new lands. The forcibly displaced Sámi watch over their calving reindeer day and night to make them stay in this new country. Tales are told of reindeer on the southern shore of Duortnosjávri in the twenties and thirties, gazing northward over the waves but unable to cross the sealike lake. Their ear markings show that they belong to families who have lost their reindeer on the forced trek southward. Being creatures of habit, reindeer stream northward in large numbers. They are like migrating birds, returning to their calving grounds and the scent of grass along the coast.

Reindeer whose ear markings show they belong to displaced families are found throughout Norrbotten county all the way to Jáhkotnjárga and the other peninsulas along the Atlantic seaboard. Once the convention has taken effect, the Norwegians have zero tolerance for any reindeer turning up in the wrong area at the wrong time of year. The Lapp Authority administers fines, handing them out on a collective basis. Any reindeer that return to their old haunts, now off-limits, are shot.

We have an old *áiti* by my parents' wooden cabin whose rusty-red paint bears signatures carved by various relatives over the years. My great-grandfather's sleds, a whole *ráidu*, have been stored here for many years. There's a lingering scent of pine tar from the harnesses, mingled with a hint of mold. The timber is covered in a dry white film. Running my hands over the wood, I feel the outline of the mark my *máttaráddjá* incised with his knife in lieu of a signature.

My *áddjá*'s family was forced to move from Talma to Laevas in 1926. This is the other branch of my forcibly relocated family, but oddly enough I recognize only now that they, too, were forcibly displaced. Maybe that's because people often speak of the forced displacements as if they applied only to "the Karesuando Sámi," even though they affected all Sámi herding communities in the far north. The vast majority were displaced from Könkämä, but in the late 1920s the County Administrative Board also reduced the population of the Sámi communities of Lainiovuoma, Sarivuoma, and Talma. The forced relocations more or less halved the Talma community.

In 1930, the issue of the losses and conflicts arising from forced displacement is raised in the Swedish Parliament. Carl Lindhagen, a Social Democrat, tables a motion calling for Sweden to remedy the unsatisfactory state of affairs resulting from "the immigration of the Karesuando Lapps." The response now states officially that the people concerned have not moved of their own free will. They are people who, "in order to comply with the authorities' orders, have had to abandon the pasturelands and migration trails they know, their extended families, their friends and the conditions they were accustomed to, and who have been obliged to sell off much of their property in haste." Awareness of the forced displacements does not lead to any further debate or put an end to further forced displacements.

On the contrary, 1930 is the year when the Lapp Authority seems to have lost all patience with the reindeer herders' constant delaying tactics. In a few years' time, the Lapp bailiffs threaten to impose coercive measures on all families who have stopped somewhere along the way. The first families reach their new Sámi herding communities in 1931. None of them have succeeded in their attempts to stay near relatives in Norrbotten, closer to home.

9

Dat lávii juoigat Sárevuomi
How the Joiking Faded Away

ON THE WAY TO GÁVTSJÁVRRIE, APRIL 1931
Iŋggá Biette ja Čuoigi Elle Gáren
Per Tomasson Skum and Helena Skum

Iŋggá Biette curses. "It's heavy going this time, that's for sure." He's experienced many spring migrations, each different, but this is something new. If you take your eyes off the reindeer for an instant, they turn back. The reindeer are nervous and hard to control. They can hardly ever stop to rest. They are losing tired calves born last year as the young animals lag behind.

The first half of the journey went better, more or less all the way from the forests around Jiellevárre to Mörttjärn. Then came the rain. Now it's pouring and the snow is turning to slush. In barely a day the ground has become soggy and porous. The animals' hooves sink into the mush. It's hard work during the day, and at night everything freezes solid. By the early hours of the morning, the ice crust is so hard and smooth that it gleams at first light like a silver spoon. The reindeer begin to forage for lichen hanging from the fir trees, spreading out when they reach a clearing.

The forest is full of big forest reindeer with unfamiliar ear markings. Small herds. Stray reindeer. The reindeer bells tinkle, attracting these strangers. They have to stop in a wet hay meadow to separate all the reindeer that don't belong to them from their herd.

121

How much farther do they have to go?

Not until north of Málege are the south-facing slopes free of snow.

"We've covered nearly a hundred kilometers now, without a break or rest," says Duommá, or Partapuoli, as they mostly call him. Partapuoli, married to Iŋggá Biette's cousin Iŋgá, is also a cousin of Elle Gáren, Iŋggá Biette's wife. Although he wrote letters to the Lapp Authority for years to avoid resettlement, that didn't save them from their current situation.

Iŋggá Biette and Partapuoli discuss what to do. What if they let the draft reindeer return to the herd and send their sleds on by road? The geldings are worn-out. They find a truck in Málege to transport their belongings, pack a bag of meat and bread, and press their clothes down into sacks.

Iŋggá Biette is accompanied by Nils Duommá, his eldest son. Though the lad has to work like a grown man, he doesn't complain. He's proud of his new factory-made skis, which are a very recent gift and don't have a scratch on them. It was that day when the county governor dropped by to see how the journey was going: strolling about in his ankle-length coat, he eyed Nils Duommá's handmade skis, passed down to him by another relative. "Bit long for a youngster like you, aren't they?" The very next day, a motorcar came by with a new pair of skis, courtesy of the *máhearra*.

Nils Duommá carefully stands them on end each time they stop.

The reindeer herd follows the roads. Once they bear westward, the journey becomes easier. The rivers are wild torrents. Around Malå-Vännäs it starts to pour again. The red pom-pom on Iŋggá Biette's *cuipi* hangs heavily. The rain plasters down reindeer fur. Partapuoli sets off in pursuit of some runaways, and it's a while before he returns, still empty-handed. "They made off over a river," he says. That's another forty animals gone.

Another sixty disappear in Gargnäs. Partapuoli returns with

twenty of them; he couldn't track the rest. Iŋggá Biette curses the state of the snow, eaten away by the downpour.

The last leg of the journey to Suorssá is snow free. Nils Duommá carries his skis along the road.

In Suorssá, their wives, Iŋgá and Elle Gáren, listen to their news about the journey. "There's hardly a herd left. They've lost . . ." Iŋgá's mouth is like a pencil stroke, as she bites her upper lip. Elle Gáren will always remember the way Iŋgá looked at her. "My half brother and Duommá must have been mad to make this journey." Iŋgá had no desire to come here.

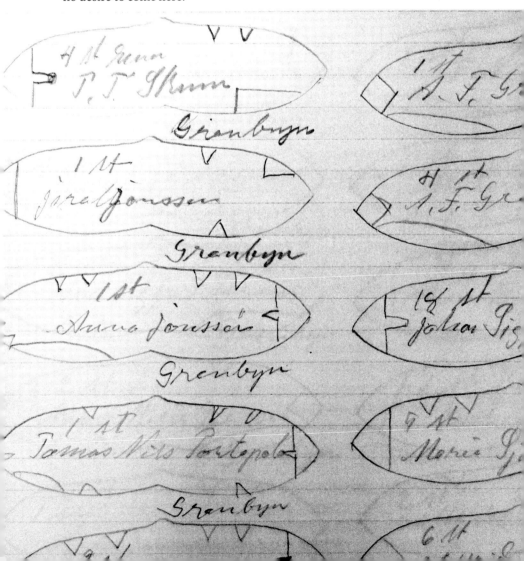

The two women came by train with their children. They loaded up the *ráidu* so as to set off for Fjällåsen station in good time. Elle Gáren dressed the youngest in flowered *gáktis* over their *ráffedorka*. She wore an apron made of the same fabric, with the key to the *giisá* attached to her belt. Her eldest daughter, Inger Ánná, can speak Swedish. She bought their tickets and translated for them. Elle Gáren kept her copper coffee pot at the top of her sack and went to buy coffee in Bastuträsk when the train stopped.

She's aware of Inger Ánná watching her from time to time. My daughter's at a sensitive age, thinks Elle Gáren. It's hardest for her because she's old enough to understand what's going on. Inger Ánná knows the Lapp bailiff wasn't the only one who wanted them out. The reindeer herders in the Sámi communities around Jiellevárre also complained about their staying there. It was hard on Inger Ánná, not being able to stay behind with her boyfriend, her cousins, her new friends. They had managed to spend five years there, long enough to put down at least some roots. Now the children will have to change school again. "*Livččii veahá lágabut . . .* ," says Inger Ánná. If they had stayed in Jiellevárre, they would have been a bit closer to home.

Elle Gáren thought they would find a hotel room in Suorssá or at least be able to rent a small bakehouse or some such place. Her son, Biette, recalls his mother's shock when they arrived in the village. "They led us to a stable; it was state property. That's where they put us. There were nine of us in our family alone, with *enná* and my sisters and brothers, and then there were Partapuoli's wife, Iŋgá, and his son, Johán, as well. Eleven of us, in a stable."

They walk in through the broad wooden doors. The children climb up on the wooden partitions. Elle Gáren tries to brush off the stalks that stick to their hide garments, their caps. The soles of her damp reindeer hide shoes are black—her delicate, carefully tailored shoes with their fine stitching. The children play at being horses

124

and feed each other with hay. She can't very well stop them playing, thinks Elle Gáren. It's a good thing they don't understand why they're not allowed to stay anywhere else. If only the Lapp inspector knew how she used to scrub the floor back home in Sohppar. How clean she kept it. It feels as if the smell is creeping in under her skin, absorbing all the air. She makes a bed for the children as far away as possible from the animals. The stable is as cold as a *goahti* with no fire, but musty and stuffy. They try to stay outdoors as much as possible.

Suorssá is a large village that reminds her a little of Vazáš with its river, its two-story houses, and the way the ice melts and breaks up. Now and then some curious person drops by. A gentle-faced man welcomes them, introducing himself as Anders Grahn. It's hard to understand the variety of Sámi he speaks. They ask Inger Ánná to speak to him in Swedish, but mostly she just says "no" in reply to all the questions he asks. She's anxious not to make a mistake. She explains that Grahn lives in Bissehis and that he's telling them about the mountains here.

The Lapp inspector, Emil Eriksson, and Ragnvald Strömgren turn up early one morning with a horse-drawn cart. They tell them they're to travel westward over the morning ice crust. The transport is provided free of charge by the Lapp Authority. They can spend the night in Eriksson's cabin in Kraddsele.

Elle Gáren and Iŋá are relieved. There will be proper beds and a stove there. They brought their worn Finnish hymnbook with them. Little Rihtta and Elle Gáren sing together: "*On porti auki. Katsokaa, se hohtaa kirkauta . . .*" Rihtta stands tall when the gentlemen praise her: "What a fine voice she has, your little girl."

While the family travels by horse-drawn cart, the reindeer herd continues to follow the river. Another forty females disappear. Sometimes Partapuoli returns with a few, but most head north, as if

125

following ropes set out to guide them. They ask the Lapp inspector for permission to let the females calve in a place where they can keep the herd together. He shakes his head: they have already been assigned calving grounds. Partapuoli is silent. He and Iŋggá Biette can see they haven't been allotted a place naturally suited to the purpose.

In the first week of May they lose reindeer while crossing the Vindelälven River. A further 250 reindeer head back where they have come from. Their tracks lead northward. Heavily pregnant females have disappeared, meaning they lost several years' income from all the calves that would have been born. Biette hears the story when they arrive at Gávtsjávrrie. "The poor creatures made off in all directions. Geldings, bulls. All of them headed north. The geldings grunted and off they went. Then they were gone. They know they're strangers in this land, you see. They're bent on going back to their own country."

The family travels on to Gieråjvvie. "We put up the *goahti* on the other side of the mountains. That's where we spent our first summer and spring." In summer Biette fingers the ears they saved from calf marking. "We don't have many reindeer left . . ."

Elle Gáren doesn't know how to thank the people who help them. They can lodge in Wilhelm Forsvall's long brewhouse, and Yngve Forsvall lets them buy goods on credit at his store. Georg Jonsson sells them a hut with a loft. Elle Gáren and Iŋggá Biette make up a story for their children about everything they've been given. She learns how to do magic with food, but it's harder with other necessities: wadmal, cloth for aprons, and shoes. She mends, darns, launders, and rushes about like the wind to make things nice for them, despite everything. Luckily there are plenty of fish in the lake.

Elle Gáren uses such words as she can cobble together to thank people in Swedish, but she's never found it particularly easy to learn

Kungl. Maj:ts Befallningshavande
i Norrbottens län

Landskansliet N:o L. 11/28.

Fol. 184 N:r 259
Ink. till Lappfogdekontoret
i Umeå d. 29 DEC. 1932

Till lappfogden i Västerbottens län.

Angående begäran från Per Tomasson Skum i Grans lappby om viss
penninghjälp.

Framställningen avser bidrag för hopsamling och överfö-
rande till Västerbotten av renar som vid avfärden från Gällivare
icke kommit med. För överflyttningen till Västerbotten av Skum, hans
husfolk, bohag och renar har statsverket fått utgiva betydande be-
lopp utöver de flyttningsbidrag som av Kungl.Maj:t bestämts och
varmed andra lappar i liknande förhållanden fått reda sig. På grund
härav och då det synes tämligen osäkert, huruvida Skum med ett even-
tuellt beviljat bidrag skulle visa sig förmå genomföra hopsamling-
en och överflyttningen av de kvarlämnade renarna, finner Länsstyrelsen vidare påkostningar från statens sida i detta fall icke böra
komma i fråga. Det torde för övrigt vara ett tämligen ofruktbart
företag att så lång väg föra ned ett jämförelsevis ringa antal renar, vilka hava en känd benägenhet för att dra sig tillbaka till
sina gamla trakter. Det synes Länsstyrelsen därför lämpligast att
Skum lämnar bemyndigande för lappväsendets tjänstemän att sälja de
renar han har kvar här i länet, varefter han kan använda försälj-
ningsbeloppen för inköp av livrenar i sin nuvarande hemtrakt. Be-
styret med hopsamling och försäljning kommer icke att kosta honom
något.

Detta meddelas Eder för kännedom och benägen åtgärd samt
Skums underrättande. Luleå i landskansliet den 27 december 1932.

foreign languages. Whenever there's no church service, she holds her own at eleven o'clock each Sunday morning. They have churches here, too, but it's not like in the north. It's a milder kind of faith. The children know they mustn't work on Sundays: the only exception is working with the reindeer. God have mercy on anyone who sets a fishing net. Elle Gáren holds on to her faith: whatever happens, the choice isn't theirs to make. She instills this in their children. "God gives, and God takes away."

At school, some children whisper that they're thieves from the north. That the northern Lapps have long fingers. That they should go back home where they belong. That things were different before they came. Iŋggá Biette is the first to suffer from homesickness. A stranger is like a strange dog, he says. "You know how it is with a strange dog. All the others crowd in on it."

Back home, they were described as very *juoigalaš*—a family known for joiking—but Iŋggá Biette has barely joiked at all since they got here. It's as if the words catch in his throat or the wind cannot carry them. He'll joik only when he meets someone from back home or when there's no one to hear. His pipe hangs permanently from the corner of his mouth. The dark forest weighs heavily on his spirits. There's no air among those firs. The calves he would have marked in summer are now somewhere between Västerbotten and Sárevuopmi.

"Only half of my reindeer were left. Think of it, only half . . . I know all about ill luck, not just the good side of life."

In the years that follow, he often wonders why they meekly obeyed the bailiffs when they assigned people to other areas.

"We were fools; we should at least have sued the County Administrative Board for sending us away and making us lose our reindeer. They should at least have been made to pay."

"We left so much behind. Dad had a big house in Soppero, you see, a wooden house. In Nedre Soppero, it was. There was a spacious room, a bedroom, and a hallway. At the other end there was a separate room and a kitchen, where a shoemaker used to live, as I recall. Mam and my cousin Inger Anna used to scrub the floor. And it was cold, there wasn't any electric heater, just a stove. I came home from school only on Saturdays, because it was over fifteen kilometers away. And there were reindeer tracks everywhere, which was handy for us—we could follow them as we ran home.

When we were told we had to leave, *áhče* wanted to sell out. The local authority bought the house for a family who lived in Övre Soppero. Dad didn't get that much for it, as far as I know, but then he probably didn't ask for much . . .

It was exciting for me, a big adventure—I was so young. We moved to Gällivare first. I went to school, as I wasn't that old. Britta was born there. But then we moved on to Ammarnäs . . . It was miserable for Mam and Dad. It really was. No fun at all. It wasn't until we got to Ammarnäs that I really started to think about what had happened. I remember there were people who looked down on us for being poor . . . And later on things got better, and we were seen as being worth more than when we arrived. I remember . . . We weren't at all like the others, I mean the Sámi families who'd lived there for a long time, who belonged in Västerbotten. We weren't like them. But there were people who helped us from the very beginning, people Mam and Dad got on well with."

Inger Anna Johansson, eldest daughter of Elle Gáren
and Iŋggá Biette, forcibly relocated from Sárevuopmi
to the Sámi herding community of Gran, 1931

130

"I had a brother who was killed skiing, when he ran into a pine tree, he was sixteen . . . and two brothers who drowned one summer. God help me, I've never forgotten that and I never will, both my oldest and my youngest brother . . . But life must go on . . . That's how it is. *Enná* used to cry a little, then it would pass; she had so much going on around her with her family. But my father couldn't get over it. He grieved, my *áhče*. He was the silent type, you see; he couldn't bring himself to weep. He used to talk about them, and what do you think he said? 'Why were we forced to come down here? If we'd stayed up north they'd still be alive today.' He'd suffered a great deal in his life and he was ailing in his last years. It started when the boys drowned.

As he grew older he'd stand and joik . . . Sárevuomi, his homeland. We had a tent, a *goahti* we'd set up in the place where we spent our winters, and once I went over to it because I could hear there was someone inside, smoking meat. I heard him joiking, and it was more beautiful than you can imagine. 'Ah,' I said, 'so that's where you are . . .'

He was joiking Sárevuomi that time, I think."

Iŋggá Biette Susánná
Susanna Andersson, youngest daughter
of Elle Gáren and Iŋggá Biette

In dal vuolgán Čokču guoran
nu guhká go sohkar njálmmis suttai

I didn't leave Čokču's side
as long as the sugar melted in my mouth

muhto vuosttas dat son lei gal mii oarjjás leŋgii
de vulggii goit buori maŋŋái

   Allet vuolgge, allet vuolgge dan buori ohcat
   dat dat lei goit jándora guoraldahkan

but once it was time he harnessed up
and left in search of good

   Don't leave, don't leave, searching for better
   all the live-long day

        Iŋggá Biette luohti
        Iŋggá Biettes joik

The registers that once stood in the old Racial Biology Institute are nearly half a meter tall. They contain various racial indices and definitions of brachycephaly (short-headedness) and dolichocephaly (long-headedness). Records of the width of a person's face, the diameter of a cranium. I leaf through the registers to the portraits and the lists of individuals. The last time I came here to conduct interviews, I heard about how some families were subjected repeatedly to racial biology examinations. The racial biologists examine them in the north, before their forced relocation, and again farther south, after the journey. They photograph them from the front and in profile. Naked, serious faced, their mouths closed. I have to know if they have got my family—and I find them.

The list of people displaced from Gárasavvon in 1921 includes my *máttaráhkku* Risten and my paternal grandfather's sister. Risten has a cranial index of 87. *Váre* is one of the people measured in Jåhkåmåhkke, after his forced relocation. They, like others, were measured both in the north and after their journey to the south. I don't know if there are any photographs of them without clothes, and right now it's more than I can bear to look into that. Would I even recognize them without their clothes on?

Iŋggá Biette and Elle Gáren's family are also subjected to racial biology examinations on two occasions, the second in 1932. At the same time, having lost much of his herd, Iŋggá Biette writes to request a loan for the purchase of reindeer. He also applies for a grant so he can round up the animals he has lost. The County Administrative Board writes: "The state has already been obliged to spend considerable sums above and beyond the transfer grant established by His Royal Majesty, with which other Lapps in similar circumstances have had to content them-selves, on the transfer to Västerbotten of Skum, his household, his household goods, and his reindeer." In the authorities' view, forcing the family to relocate has already cost them quite enough money.

They are at their harshest in their treatment of the Kemi family, who have held out against forced displacement for some years. The Kemis are originally from the Finnish side of the border, but like many oth-ers they become Swedish citizens once the borders close. After several lean years, they settle in the forests around Sohppar and Vazáš.

As forest Sámi, they do not rank highest on the Lapp Authority's scale. Sweden has been trying for some time to put a stop to reindeer husbandry in the forests. Under the country's "Lapps should remain Lapps" policy, only mountain Sámi are viewed as genuine, so policy is focused on accommodating reindeer herding in the mountains where feasible. Moreover, the Kemi brothers have refused to join a Sámi reindeer herding community. They appeal and refuse to leave.

Are those who resist penalized? Or is the County Administrative Board just adamant that forced relocations must be enforced, come what may? The Kemis are the only family in the Swedish part of Sápmi to undergo forced displacement twice within a short period of time. Their reindeer herd is forcibly driven south between 1930 and 1931. But the reindeer turn back, and the family follow them, returning to their home region around Sohppar. On 5 December 1931, the Lapp bailiff writes that since they "have so far failed to make even the slightest attempt to prepare for the prescribed relocation, I would respectfully propose that the County Administrative Board establish the amount due in fines and authorize me to set in motion, without further ado, the forced slaughter of part of the herd owned by Niko-laus Nilsson Kemi and Johan Nilsson Kemi."

With this threat hanging over them, the family migrate of their own accord in the spring of 1932.

Till Konungen   2 c   Na 2½

Biret Anne

Aarbuor Nils

Hearra lappfogden

4/4. 1929

Sedan då vi genom nyhetstidningarne fått
vetskap om att Norrbottens läns länsstyrelse
har gjord förklaring, angående vår tvångs-
flyttningsak, får vi härmed ännu med största
underdånighet åberopa följande. För det första att
vi finge bo på samma plats där vi själva och våra
renar ha uppväxt som vi förut har anfört, nådig
anhållas. För det andra om till det ingen möj-
lighet finnes, ändock, att vi få bo i det av Länsstyrelsen
nämnda Killangi skogslappby, vilket är emellan
Lainijoki och Lainiälven öster om landsvägen Soppero-
Killangi
Fm n. 58.

nej!
(28 na s. 2 m.fl. ställen)

det hör
de ej (se
28 na. s. 2)

10

Amas riikkas
A Strange Land

MARCH 1932
The Kemi family

Things seem as usual, like an ordinary seasonal migration. Lásse lies
in the *rissla* drawn by the first reindeer in the *ráidu* led by Ánna, his
mother. He's bundled up snugly under a hide, his breath forming
puffs of cold mist. Lásse has pride of place in the *ráidu*, lying on a
broad reindeer hide, and Ánna has tucked him in under a *roavgu*, a
motley cover cobbled together from several woolly sheepskins. Only
his face can be seen. Lulled to sleep by the creaking of the sled on
the snow and the tinkling of bells, he's comfortable enough. Baby
Elle, swaddled and laced into her cradle, looks sound asleep. Once
she's in her *gietkka*, she rarely bothers anyone, as long as she's snug
and has something to eat. Lásse hardly notices her cry. Nothing out
of the ordinary there.

He watches them clearing the ground for the *goahti*, knowing
he'll have to wait awhile. That's the high point of the day, crawling
inside into the warmth and lying down. Being handed a cup of hot
coffee. The *goahti* protects them against the wind, the darkness, and
everything that can't be seen. The fire's already lit when he goes
in. He gets the dog to lie down in the *loaidu* and positions himself
between the fire and the animal's warm body. Lásse and Nilsá often
quarrel over who gets to lie next to the dog, and each claims him
once the other has nodded off, but Lásse's brother isn't here now.

2⅓. ua.

enär andra lappar sådana som vi, tillåtes att utan
någon tvånghet bo där, trots av det att äro y ursprungliga
skogslappar, som exempelvis bröder hr Mangus
vilkas fader har som molibes som vår fader
Mikkelsson Kemi
burit fjällapp, och har flyttat till skogslandet samma
tid som vår fader eller omkring 25 år sedan. Det
känns som litet personligt, när till andra likadana
personer brukas en annan lag än till andra.
Och för det tredje om det heller icke är möjlig
få vi anhålla att vi få vara fjällappar i vår faders
spår i Talma lappby i Jukkasjärvi socken och flytta
under somrarna till Norge.
Ovanstående anföra vi med största underdånighet
och hoppas vi så att vår förut gjorda långa och
besvärliga Stockholmsresa y blev utan resultat

Soppero den 4 april 1929

Underdånigt

Johan Nilsson Kemi   Nikolaus Nilsson Kemi

The older siblings have been allowed to stay behind with their *siessá* in Sohppar. They may as well stay on at the Láttevárri school, he's heard his parents say.

The flames writhe in the *árran*. The *goahti* looks just as usual, with each item in its allotted place. The coffee pot, one side of which is sootier than the other, stands with its spout pointing inward. The precious coffee vapors will then flow into the *goahti*'s inner sanctum, not out through the door. Lásse's mother, Ánna, is sitting in the *goahti*'s furthest reaches, beside the *boaššu*. The only thing different from usual is her tears. "She keeps crying, our Mam, off and on."

He thinks of those coffee cups. They set up the *goahti* between Málbmavárri and Jiellevárre and tethered the draft reindeer to some half-grown pines. His mother was supposed to take a reindeer over to the storekeeper.

"Come along if you like," she said to Lásse. The mere idea gave him butterflies. He'd never seen a place bigger than Vazáš or Badje Sohppar.

The storekeeper had everything. Flour. Coffee. Sugar. Cloth. China. Lásse stuck close to Ánna while she selected half a dozen delicate china cups. She meant to keep them in her *gohppogiisá* and take them out when visitors dropped by. The storekeeper packed them into a bag, one by one. "Can I carry them, Mam?" Ánna nodded, handing him the bag. On the way back to the *rissla*, it was as if the bag suddenly acquired a life of its own. It slipped out of his hands, clinking as it hit the packed snow. "That's what I remember most, those cups. Nothing special about them as far as I was concerned, but Mam . . . well, she wasn't at all happy."

There are several Sámi herding communities between Sohppar and the forests south of Jiellevárre. Their new grazing lands are in the forests west of Nahtavárre. Lásse sees only trees and bogs. They're going to pass five herding communities: Gábna, Laevas, Girjás,

Baste, and Unna tjerusj. "Our dad and Uncle Nils went on ahead with the reindeer herd, and we followed them."

Uncle Nils drives the reindeer with the dogs' help. They are *giedavuol*, as the expression goes, responsive to his every wish. Uncle Nils is good with animals. Every day, his wife, Biret Ánne, serves the dogs their portion of *gilis*, a hodgepodge of sinews and blood she's cooked up for them. The dogs are the first to be fed. Their barking is like a lullaby to the children in the *rissla*, a song reassuring them that all is well with the journey.

They have been forced to move to new country twice, this being the second time. Though Lásse took part the first time, he can't remember anything about it. His father was in the hospital with a burst appendix at the time. He's shown Lásse the scar, which runs halfway across his abdomen. Because Lásse's parents had protested against the move, the officials engaged other reindeer herders to drive their herd cross-country. The family looked on while other people rounded up their reindeer and drove them off. Lásse's father has told him all about it—or maybe it was Uncle Nils or Biret Ánne. "Each herding community had a man responsible for welcoming them when they arrived. And it went on like that. There'd be another in the next herding community. When they reached this region, the Purnu group met them and helped them travel on toward Muttos." All of this cost 533.20 kronor. The story goes that the travelers had to have reindeer from their herds slaughtered along the way, but who knows if that's true.

The family took the train. Disembarking at Nahtavárre station, they barely knew where they had arrived, whether they were on their head or their feet. An unknown forest is impenetrable. Guarding the reindeer was the devil's own job: they would turn and head back, and there was no keeping them together. Nils would race after them in panic, but he didn't get very far. The reindeer wandered off across bogs the size of lakes, snow bridges covering treacherous

140

terrain, and stretches of melting ice that were impassable for humans.

The Lapp Authority wasn't convinced that the Kemi brothers hadn't lost their reindeer on purpose. They questioned villagers to find out what had happened. The Rosenbergs from Ruodna bore witness that the Kemis hadn't purposely lost reindeer or been negligent. "It is next to impossible for a person to cross these streams when they are at their highest level in spring," they wrote in defense of the Kemi family.

The Kemis returned home, but the Lapp Authority threatened to slaughter their reindeer herd by order unless they traveled south again.

This time they refuse to let the powers that be drive their reindeer south. They leave of their own accord.

The Lapp Authority builds a corral on a mountain surrounded by bogs the size of seas. The tapping of hammers can be heard far and wide. Slender saplings and spindly trees are felled and nailed to pines, the nails hammered straight into the bark of trees so thick that a man can't even encircle the trunk with his arms. The building goes on for days, meter by meter. It's the biggest enclosure Lásse has ever seen, so vast that it would take an hour or so to walk all the way around the outside. The curved tips of his hide shoes sometimes get stuck in the cracks when he clambers up on the fence. The Lapp bailiff has taken on extra workers at the Kemi family's expense. After all, he says, it's the Kemis' own corral, and they're going to get a 200-kronor loan. Though neither Johan nor Nils likes running up debt, it beats losing their reindeer again. Lásse's father says they wouldn't manage without the enclosure. "You can't keep reindeer on strange land without using a corral." This is the first time their calves will be born inside an enclosure.

Ánna and Biret Ánne search for a suitable spot to erect the *goahti* and choose a dry slope beside a large bog, near the way out

141

of the corral. Lásse has never seen such trees: snag pines and broad, twisted *Pinus sylvestris*. Like *stállu* against the sky. These pines are draped with dry, spindly branches that become entangled and break off. Closer to the bog, copses of firs alternate with marshy pits.

As the ground inside the corral gets too churned up, they begin to let the reindeer out during the day. The animals sink into the swampy pits and struggle to free themselves. "There are acid bogs all around here, great big mires. Uncle Nils and Dad have to pull reindeer up out of the muck every day."

Puffing on their pipes, Lásse's father and his uncle Nils gaze at the dense forest. The past few years they've had their reindeer calve at Divru, an area of low mountain around Sohppar with trees so puny that they can't keep out the wind. "Hellishly dark" is how Johan describes the new forest. "It feels personal when there's one law for some and another law for the rest."

Ánna gathers wood, fetches water, kneads dough. At least they have firewood. Lásse sees her closing in on herself. "Now and then I see Mam crying, but what can you do when you're just a little boy?"

Ánna's never been much of a storyteller. It's Biret Ánne who knows all the tales, the kinship networks, and how everything in the world is interconnected. She tells Lásse how the rain lashed down around Njálmmesgorsu the day he was born. And there's the tale of Johan's journey to meet the king and entreat his mercy. That was in the winter of 1929. They had been trying to appeal against the relocation order for several years. When nothing worked, they decided to seek an audience with the "father of the country" and beg him to take mercy on them. Johan bought a rail ticket to the capital, taking a *verdde* from Važáš with him as an interpreter. One Saturday in January they arrived in a foggy Stockholm. Wearing his shoes of white reindeer hide, Johan slid through the slippery streets of the capital. His *verdde* borrowed a *beaska* to wear over his suit, concealing

142

DAGENS NYHETER.

LÖSNUMMERPRIS: 15 ÖRE
(Å JÄRNVÄGARNA 20 ÖRE)
TRYCKERI: DAGENS NYHETER, STOCKHOLM

Måndagen den 7 Januari 1929

Stockholmssuppl. nr 20934

CRNER.

Känslan

för ansvaret bättre än lag eller tvärtom.

Sakkunskapen om körkorten.

Uppifrån: hovrättsrådet J. Alsén, ombudsman J. Mårdh och kapten A. Norlander.

Det råder litet delade meningar bland 1927 års motorfordonssakkunniga om behovet att skärpa de medicinska fordringarna för erhållandet av körkort. D:r P. G. Olssons förslag i den frågan, som detaljerat återgavs i gårdagens tidning, har rönt lidande känslor hos kommittén — där är egentligen bara en i sak som man är rikligt enig om, och det är att d:r Olsson i sin måna varit ute i ogjort väder då han klandrat kommittén för att den i sitt

Forts. å sista sidan.

---

ning

ares

ben

olan.

hota lockad.

stens polissko-
arscherna ela-
t framsträckta
illigt annat i
kt en våldsam
depterna, som
de i en amper
tens kärlidnin-
även andra
och med att
anstalten, om
arare, som äro
bli elevastrejk,
i den utarbetade
m, säger man.

mnastikläraren
. Han beteck-
kall, enär han
i en motorlans-
iliga undervis-
 bestå i att
lisa, civilt och
 mest fröjdar
na armen och
na modernyker
ren''.

 sista sidan.

D:r G. HALLDÉN.

Idrotten

ger ungdom bra hållning och god anda

Bättre bostäder tuberkulosbot.

Bättre bostäder är det bästa botemedlet i kampen mot tuberkulosen, och gymnastik och idrott äro oumbärliga för de ungas sunda utveckling, framhåller förste provinsialläkaren i Älvsborgs län i sitt svar på Dagens Nyheters enquête om hälsotillståndet och den allmänna hygienen i riket.

I Älvsborgs län har hälsotillståndet under året varit gott. Epidemiska sjukdomar ha förekommit sparsamt, endast beträffande scharlakansfeber torde en ringa ökning av frekvensen kunna påvisas.

De veneriska sjukdomarna visa en bestämd tendens till ökad utbredning. Den kraftiga tillbakagången av dessa sjukdomar, som kunde konstateras efter ikraftträdandet av Lex veneris, torde således icke helt böra tillskrivas verkningarna av denna lag. Bidragande orsaker torde ha varit penningvärdets stigande under kristiden och i många fall tillämpandet av restriktionslagstiftningen.

Tuberkulosen är fortfarande vår enda smittosamma folksjukdom av större betydelse. Dödligheten i denna sjuk-

Forts. å sista sidan.

Bioboven

på Imperial fast och förd till Långbro.

Byråchefen såg Klaranidingen.

Kriminalpolisen lyckades på söndagen få ett snabbt slut på affären i biografen Imperial. Den man som hotat kassörskan med dragen kniv infångades tidigt på morgonen i Täby. På eftermiddagen var hela saken utagerad. Förövaren av dådet, en 40-årig gårdfarihandlande Bernhard August Karlsson, visade sig identisk med en periodiskt sinnessjuk, som vårdats på olika hospital alltsedan 1914. Han hade nu fått ett svårartat återfall, och överfördes redan på söndagskvällen till Långbro. Någon vidare åtgärd mot honom kommer icke att företagas. Beträffande nidingen från Klara, måleriarbetaren Erik Rosenius, har Dagens Nyheter vid ett samtal med byråchefen Eric Wijlmark i fångvårdsstyrelsen inhämtat att hans fall med all sannolikhet kommer att remitteras till interneringsnämnden. Om så sker blir mannen alldeles säkert hänvisad till anstalten för förminskat tillräkneliga, en internering som kan komma att gälla livstid. Vidare avslöjade byråchefen att det var han som gav polisen uppslaget till att Rosenius skulle vara den skyldige till misshandeln i Klaraskolan.

Karlsson konfronterad med kassörskan.

Kassörskan på Imperialbiografen gavs på söndagsmiddagen tillfälle att närmare skärskåda den infångade Bernhard Karlsson och kunde därvid ögonblickligen identifiera honom som samme man, vilken hotat henne i biljettkassan. Karlsson såg icke kassörskan vid hennes besök i polishuset men kände sig fortfarande då samma sätt som på Imperial. Han skulle nödvändigt visa sina ärr, vilka han påstod sig ha inte bara i huvudet, och vidare yttrade han någonting om att han var ''Bernhard Karlsson från Svea land''.

Det låg alltså i öppen dag att mannen var sinnessjuk. D:r Eneström, polisens undersökningsläkare i fall som dessa, kunde också omedelbart efter sin undersökning konstatera att mannen erhållit ett återfall i sin sinnessjukdom. Alltsedan 1914 har han i olika etapper varit intagen på sinnessjukhus. Två gånger har han suttit på Konradsberg samt en gång på vardera Gibraltar i Göteborg och Långbro. Från Långbro utskrevs Karlsson sista gången 1927. Han har dock aldrig tidigare under sin sinnessjukdom uppträtt på sätt som nu skett, varför det är anledning anta att hans tillstånd förvärrats i hög grad. Mannen är gift och har ett minderårigt barn.

Forts. å sista sidan.

N. F. JOHANSSON och J. NILSSON.

Två Vittangilappar be för sitt renbete, söka konungens nåd.

Stockholm har för närvarande besök av två lappar som rest den långa vägen hit från Vittangi i Norrbottens län för att personligen uppvakta konungen i en invecklad renbetesangelägenhet. De båda männen startade sin färd hit på torsdagsmorgonen i 20 graders köld, och på lördagskvällen anlände de till Centralen, där de möttes av Londondimma. Med försiktiga steg tassade de i sina lapskor i väg till sitt logi över de glaserade gatorna.

De båda renkararna äro Johan Nilsson-Kemi, skogslapp från Vittangi vidsträckta socken, och nybyggaren och sakföraren N. F. Johansson, desslikes lapp, från samma domän och den för-

res juridiska biträde, tolk och talesman vid den blivande uppvaktningen. Det förhåller sig nämligen så att Johan Nilsson-Kemi, som för resten endast talar lapska och finska, och hans bröder Nikolaus, vilka tillsammans äro ägare av trehundra renar och i hela sitt liv varit bofasta skogslappar i om ett område av ungefär en kvadratmil vidd i Vittangi socken, av vederbörande lappfogde och ock så av länsstyrelsen och regering ålagts att flytta till annan trakt, ett område som samvaras inom en trakt, ett område som också är länsstyrelsen emellertid synnerligen svårt att finna sig uti, det skulle

Forts. å sista sidan.

TVÅ

utställningar och två slags söndagsminer.

Det var skratt och munterhet i Konstakademien i går, där omkring 500 personer infunnit sig för att titta på Albert Engströms gubbar. Mot den glada gruppen till vänster bildar den mitt emot en verkningsfull kontrast. Det allvarliga sällskapet fotograferades

everything but his tie and his freshly polished shoes. They obtained an audience with the king, and they told him that the mountains, lakes, and streams they knew had "such a place in their hearts that relocation to the Gällivare area is like moving to Siberia."

But the royal audience proved of no avail either, Biret Ánne says. "Came to nothing." Siberia meant nothing to the king. Uncle Nils made an attempt to hand over all his reindeer to Biret Ánne, if she was permitted to remain in the north. That proved impossible, too.

In Lásse's recollections, it's always his father who travels to meetings and visits people. Uncle Nils is more of a loner. He won't leave the forest. He wants to stay beside the herd, follow its movements. Listen to the reindeer bells, move the animals around, gather them together. That's why Nils is the one whose reindeer have thrived best. He has been blessed with animals bearing magnificent antlers and with females the size of geldings.

Their reindeer find plenty of forage in the mires and forests but continue to head off northward all the time. Once the mosquitoes arrive, it becomes even harder to keep hold of them. During the summer they light smoky fires to protect the reindeer from insects. They choose the sites of the fires so that the wind blows the smoke in the right direction. The older children dig up peat. When they lay peat and moss on the fire, the smoke billows out as if from a forest fire. The smell is acrid. All Lásse has to do is help with the firewood. Gradually they become accustomed to the omnipresent swarms of mosquitoes. Horseflies cluster on the seams of their *gáktis* if they're still for a moment.

"Sit still, and they won't bite you," his mother admonishes him.

Ánna keeps four or five females to milk. The sleeves of her *gákti* are rolled up and rumpled. When the rich milk coats the fabric, she rinses it out with coffee. Each drop is precious, Lásse knows. He's never allowed to taste it. Once the cloudberries have ripened, carpeting the bog, Ánna blends the fresh berries with a little creamy milk. It feels as if the taste will linger in his mouth forever. "That's the best thing I've ever eaten."

The forest is a fine place to play. The children learn tricks to find their way, such as turning right or left around every other pine tree. Lásse sometimes accompanies Ánna on her visits to the village. The people here have houses. No one apart from their family lives in a *goahti*. The forest reindeer herders have farms and meadows. Most of them speak a dialect of Finnish, though there are villages where they speak nearly the same language as Lásse's family. Ánna visits smallholders who offer her coffee in cups dark with age. Now and then they exchange a few words, and sometimes the visitors are given fish and potatoes. Grayling and perch. They're hospitable, these villagers, even though they have nothing to give away.

At home, Lásse's mother sighs now and then. She misses their home in Sohppar, where local women would drop by. Lásse hears her voice. "Oh, Lord, they're all up north, and here am I, on my own." She and Biret Ánne talk once the others have dozed off, when they think no one can hear. "It's a good thing our Mam has our uncle's missus nearby. At least they've got each other. Because the menfolk are mostly out working with the reindeer, and they get to meet other people while they're out and about." Biret Ánne's own children are nearly grown, and she helps Ánna with her little ones. Lásse recalls that hardly anyone ever drops by, only the occasional villager. "We were left to our own devices a lot, you know. But that's how it is, I suppose, you become a kind of outsider. Surely there must have been some alternative, other than the state making off with the whole reindeer herd. That's how I think as I grow older. There must have been some alternative."

"My father came to Jåhkågaska, and in the summer they moved to Låddejåhkå. It was an *oarjelsadj*: there were already other Sámi people living there. They built a small *goahti*. This is where you're to stay, the Lapp bailiff told them, but they got to missing other people from the north so badly . . . They traveled on the quiet to join their kinsfolk. They got together in Guvtjávri: my father, Biltto Ánte, Nils Orbus . . . *Isá* and Biltto Ánte lived in a *goahti* built of peat. I was already born by then . . . It was high up, above the bog, quite close to where the snow scooter track is today. We were all family together. All of us on the same spot. Then they did a flit on the quiet, to Eanonjálbme. Gathered together, in one group. People want to live close together, you see. They told the Lapp bailiff they hadn't got round to moving that year, the snow had melted so quickly . . . It melted too quickly every year.

But they never wanted to talk about it. They were in a state of shock, like people suffering from shock. They had to start again from scratch."

Orbusa Heaikka Iŋgá
Inger Partapuoli,
whose parents were forcibly transferred to the
Sámi reindeer herding community of Sirges, 1923

146

"We didn't even go to visit our relations in Arjeplog . . . Odd thing, that. Very odd, it seems to me. God only knows why not. Maybe it was such an effort to get there by train and bus, I don't know what the problem was . . . But my father would travel north once a year. *Isá* used to go up to Gällivare to see his family. He'd go every year. He used to call people in the north several times a week. He longed to be there . . .

People say we wouldn't have survived if it hadn't been for *eidde*. She was a tough one, my mother. She could cope with anything. My aunt, her sister Elle, used to say: our Iŋger Márjá's like a mountain lemming. She's not afraid of anything. *Isá* just used to joik; he'd joik all the time, whether he was lying down or whether he was sitting. And he used to call the folks up north. He wasn't happy, we knew that.

My father didn't want us to live here, and I don't know where he wanted us to go, where we were supposed to go, but he was dead set on moving. We were never supposed to learn the names of the mountains here. I don't know the name of a single valley here in Vapsten. They didn't want to be here. We weren't supposed to settle down here, we weren't supposed to accept that this was our home.

I understand now that I can live anywhere . . . I'm not sure if that's the result of trauma or what. It's a kind of . . . oh, I don't know. I just can't put down any roots. Maybe that's the wrong expression, but what I mean is, I'm not afraid of moving somewhere else or traveling. Nigá Blind used to say: wherever the reindeer go, I go too. I've never worked with reindeer in that way, but I can go anywhere, too. That does have its advantages."

Heigása Nilssá Márge
Margareta Omma, the daughter of Heigása Nilsá and
Márggu Vulle Iŋger Márjá, who finally settled in Vapsten
after many years of forced displacement

147

Guhkás šadden eret
iežán riegádan'eatnamis

de go bohten vieljain
Jåhkåmåhkkai
mon massen iežán miela

mannen guosa vuollái
vieljain vellededjen

vurden dassá bođii
mu unna vielja boazu

Far away have I come
From the place where I was born

> when I came with my brothers
> to Jokkmokk
> I lost spirit

> I crept in under a spruce tree
> with my brother I rested

> I waited for the coming
> of my little brother's reindeer

> part of a *luohti* joiked by Orbusa Nilsá,
> who was forcibly relocated to Sirges

Some distance beyond Gárasavvon's new churchyard lies the old one, occupying a dry ridge with trees creeping down to the water's edge. A flight of stone steps runs up from the road, and a sign offers to restore crosses. The ground is hummocky. Once a grave has passed a certain age, a new one has been superimposed on it. The names here are the same as those in the churchyards farther south in Sápmi. Piltto. Omma. Skum. Here lies someone's father or mother. A cousin they may never have seen again.

The women's names appear below those of their menfolk. Here, as in so many other contexts, they are subordinate to their husbands, even though many of them gave their names to large Sámi clans. Women are reindeer owners with reindeer markings of their own, yet when tracing the forced displacements in the archives you might easily fail to notice their very existence. They are referred to as "members of the household." The Lapp Authority's piles of papers contain practically no female names. Women are expected to follow their husbands into exile just as one sled follows another in a *ráidu*. A household receives an additional travel allowance of 50 kronor if the man has a wife.

I believe I can discern a pattern in all these stories. Many voices, speaking independently of each other, describe women as the most vulnerable members of their community. They stay in their *goahtis* while the men are out working together among the reindeer. They are left alone with the children while others meet at the neighboring village's reindeer corral. The women carry firewood home and hack open holes in the ice that have frozen over during the night.

Sisters and other family members who used to help each other day to day have been left behind in the north. They miss their female friends. Only many years later do they acquire telephones and start to call the folks back home.

The forced displacements take place at a time of change, when a new style of reindeer husbandry is emerging. Until the relocations, the women travel with the *ráidus*. Although it's no easy life, they share it with others and work with the reindeer, just like their menfolk. In the 1930s, however, the families start to stay at home, in permanent settlements. It is an irony of fate that this new, lonely life coincides with the forced relocations.

One of the most frequently quoted Sámi proverbs says that the downy birch doesn't break in two; it merely bends. You bear your hurt alone, for breaking down won't make your daily life any easier. Your tears should fall unseen on your shawl. This philosophy of life revolves around the word *birget*—surviving and coping. Each year the reindeer must survive the winter: that is what matters, not people's feelings.

I grew up surrounded by all this, yet I still wonder how they coped. Alone, week after week, month after month, and year upon year.

The children are invisible, too. The authorities register each child's reindeer marking and the boarding school he or she is to be packed off to on arrival at the family's new dwelling place. What the archives don't mention is the children's terror. How those who have just arrived at school scratch and claw, sobbing, their noses dripping; how, following the line of a fence, they run off into the forest and hide in trees. There's no mention of how they cry that they don't want to go to a boarding school where a foreign language is spoken. Not straight away!

How close do you hug a child who will have to spend the next six months in an unknown school, right after arriving in a new place?

Their mothers sit with them until they fall asleep, stroke their cheeks, then walk away.

All the Sámi herding communities in Västerbotten apart from Ran are obliged to take in displaced families in the end, more or less against their will. The conflicts that have arisen in Norrbotten are replicated. No one listens to the people involved; they are presented with a *fait accompli*. Those relocated under duress are loath to move, while the existing inhabitants are reluctant to take in more reindeer herders. They have to cope with the situation as best they can. The only cases in which forced relocations are not carried out are when people either become too sick to move or die before the time to move arrives.

Gusttu Bierar and Márjá arrive in Strimasund in 1932. In a final protest, they move to Umbyn, where they have friends, instead of remaining in the Sámi herding community of Gran, as ordered by the Lapp bailiff. Gusttu Bierar sends half their reindeer on in advance, to make sure they don't end up alone in another herding community.

When the new reindeer herders arrive in the Västerbotten herding communities, many of them have been on the move for five or six years. They have grown accustomed to homelessness. It's something you can't simply wash off.

"Three Lapps (Olov Andersson Omma, Per Persson Bals, and Per Gustavsson Idivuoma) are currently living in the Lapp herding community of Sirkas, in the parish of Jokkmokk, while another (Johannes Henriksson Omma, with his sons Nils and Olov) is living in the Lapp herding community of Arjeploug, in the parish of Arjeploug: all of them are on their way to the districts to which they have been assigned in Västerbotten and Jämtland. However, unfavorable grazing conditions and other circumstances have hitherto made it impracticable to effect their dislocation. Since grazing conditions are exceptionally favorable in all forests this winter, however, there is nothing to impede the implementation of the planned dislocation . . . Nonetheless, once the time has come for the said Lapps to continue their journey, they might conceivably attempt to postpone their move once again on some grounds or other, and it is therefore of the greatest importance that the authorities be empowered to effect the dislocation, even if this has to be done against the Lapps' will. In other words, it should be possible to take appropriate measures at their financial expense, should they prove refractory. As Section 39 of the Lapp Law states that this cannot be done unless the Lapps concerned have first been ordered, subject to a penalty, to take the requisite measures, I would, with all due respect, request that the County Administrative Board order each and every one of the abovementioned Lapps, subject to a penalty, to set off for the districts to which they have been assigned before the end of February of the current winter."

LAPP BAILIFF RESPONSIBLE FOR THE SOUTHERN DISTRICT OF NORRBOTTEN LULEÅ, 5 FEBRUARY 1931

Risttena Máŋá

11

Dáppe láidestit eará jienain, gilljot iežá huvkimiin

They Lead the Reindeer in a Different Language Here

STRIMASUND, JUNE 1932

Márjá walks about quietly, taking in her surroundings. She observes the position of the trees and the contours of the slope. Some of the birches are taller than the pines up north. How old are they, what have they witnessed and lived through? Angelica grows along the banks of the brook. Spotting sorrel in the undergrowth, Márjá pinches off a few delicate leaves. There's no need to walk far to pick it. It tastes of summer: tart, melting upon the tongue. The trees grow sparsely here. This is no impenetrable forest. Its leafy shade is welcoming, and the water is close by. There are bogs full of cloudberries. The children have found slender birch trees in whose branches they sway back and forth. Yet to Márjá it feels dark. No view. It's like a dense, leafy green cauldron.

She finds a boulder several meters high that will make a good storage place for provisions. Her hands feel its coolness, encircled by a shady wall of birches. At ground level there's a small hollow, ideal for keeping butter, milk, and fish cool.

Márjá and Gusttu Bierar have put up their light-colored *goahti* on a hillside not far west of Ándom Ovllá and Ristiinná.

A short way away in the opposite direction, Ándom Ovllá's cousins have set up their *goahti*. Three faint wisps of smoke are visible in the sunlight.

157

Ándom Ovllá and Ristiinná are closest to the lake. Their family occupies the right side of the *goahti,* while Biito Biera and old Mihkela Máret live in the left *loaidu.* Beside their tent stands the skeleton of a new peat *goahti,* its ribs made of birch trunks stripped of their bark. They haven't yet had the time to cover it in birch bark and peat. Biito Biera says it's "the size of a church." It's the biggest *goahti* he's ever built.

None of them have lived in their own peat *goahti* since they left the far north. For six years they've lived in tent *goahtis* in one new place after another. They managed to stay in Vájsá for several years before being forced to travel onward. Biito Biera had been so sure that the authorities would let them stay. He refused to pack until the last possible moment. "We wanted to live in Vájsá. I'd planned to stay on with my family, but Enbom threw us out. He read the law out loud to us. We had no choice. It said 'Tärnaby' in our papers. They said, if you don't leave, we'll pay other reindeer herders to drive your herd south, at your expense. They intimidated me."

Ándom Ovllá and Ristiinná's brother Ándde left with the herd, while Biito Biera followed with the *ráidu.* This time they decided not to take any dry goods with them; they could always buy provisions if necessary. All they packed was enough meat to last them until fall. The reindeer made their way southward, from the Jåhkåmåhkke area toward Lïkssjuo, then they followed the Ume-älven River westward. Biito Biera tied a hide to the back of the *ráidu,* dragging it behind the sleds to rub it clean in the snow. They've "been cheated again," he observes.

"You'll get help to send all your belongings on and to watch over your reindeer so you don't lose any of them. That's what they told me. But we had to keep watch ourselves, around the clock. They made big promises, but they didn't give us much help."

The only thing provided was a truck to take the family to their destination. The Lapp Authority paid the driver, who followed

Ándom Ovllá to pick up the women and children. Ristiinná had already packed by the time they arrived. They loaded cloth bags, hide bags, *horstaseahkat,* boxes, and sleds onto the back of the vehicle. Ristiinná tethered their puppy on top of the pile of belongings and hoisted the children up into the cabin.

The last journey—to Striima from Bårjås—was hardest. Ándom Ovllá sees that in his wife; sometimes her face is as if chiseled from wood. Ristiinná buries herself in her everyday tasks, providing food, looking after the children. She'd grown accustomed to living near her family, and she, too, had thought they'd be allowed to stay.

Márjá and Gusttu Bierar arrived last spring, a year after the others. The Lapp bailiff had granted them a year's grace to round up all their reindeer. They left their sleds in Hemavan, where Gusttu Bierar turned them upside down and piled them on top of each other. "We arrived in the spring of 1932 with our *ráidu* and reindeer herd. Over a thousand kilometers, that's how far we'd traveled with the *ráidu*."

The place where they have now gathered is called Striima. It lies at the foot of a massif known as Aartege, where Ándom Ovllá has found rock formations sculpted by water. Grassy meadows. Aartege is said to have its own joik, though none of them have heard it yet.

Ristiinná washes clothes in the brook and makes sure that everything is neat and in good repair. She hands out freshly baked loaves and packs dried meat in the girls' bags. The girls have to go off to school again, and they've grumbled about the porridge and salted herring there. The bread won't last long, but the loaves are as round as she can make them. She's heard her twin daughters talking to each other, lying under their cotton *rággas*. The thin cloth doesn't keep their anxiety at bay, nor does a *goahti* hide their tears. If they could choose to be birds, they'd have flown off in a different direction, she knows. This year the family's maid, Lánggo Márge, can't accompany the girls to school and stay with them there. "*Isá* will come with you all the way," she says.

The school, three *goahtis* in the birch forest at the foot of Atoklimpen, is a few dozen kilometers away. The girls will have to repeat their first year because their Swedish isn't up to standard. Iŋgá is due to start school this year, too. Ristiinná has heard the girls talking to their younger siblings in their broken Swedish. The twins, Elle and Márge, have been teaching the younger children the few words they know. They whisper when they think she's not listening. The words they normally use are being watered down here, fading away.

Their maid has told her how the girls have been called "dim-witted northerners" because they can't speak or understand much Swedish. They've been accused of bringing lice into the school. Ristiinná has heard the stories about other children prancing about with her girls' *suoidnevierra* on their heads. The girls themselves have told her how scared they are of the village lads who pelt them with lumps of ice and yell about Lapps.

Ándom Ovllá is silent on his return home. Once the children are asleep, he tells Ristiinná how the teacher ticked him off. "Why haven't you taught your children any Swedish?" she asked.

"How am I supposed to teach them? I can't speak Swedish, can I?"

Ándom Ovllá can read forests and mountains, but he's never got through any books.

Ristiinná thinks of her girls at school each time she tidies up the bedclothes in the place where they sleep when they're at home. As her youngest chatter away like little songbirds, she lets the sound—along with the effort of clothing and feeding the little ones and lulling them to sleep—blot out her worries. The children run about with the dogs and climb up into birch trees. They catch small fish in the brook. In front of their *goahti*, Gusttu Bierar builds a knee-high corral out of brushwood for them to play in and puts some reindeer antlers in it, a miniature herd just for the children. He teaches them how to lasso reindeer, and they pretend to mark each other's ears. Márjá tells them stories when it's time for them to rest. She's fondest of telling them about Njávešeatni and Háhcešeatni, the ancestral mothers of all that is good and evil. Njávešeatni is the daughter of the sun, and humans are the sun's children.

The summer is so stiflingly warm that the mosquitoes tire in the course of the day. The dogs seek shade, and the reindeer make their way up to the remaining patches of snow. Márjá misses the coolness of their peat *goahti*. They don't know where to take shelter. The sun is already beaming in through the door of the tent when they wake, casting shadows of trees on its fabric. The smoky air

wafts outward in the heat when they make fires to drive away insects.

Gusttu Bierar gets to know the other people in the village. Every day he picks up new Swedish words. "Chatterboxes are quick to learn," says Ándom Ovllá. Gusttu Bierar says he "misses the old lands terribly." If anyone asks Ándom Ovllá how he feels, he says he has no choice but to accept the situation. He registered for relocation of his own accord.

"I've only myself to blame." Aartege has good pasturage, and it's theirs to use. So far there have been no major conflicts between them and the other reindeer herders.

"We're separated by the river and this huge mountain. We're not so different from each other. But their reindeer are smaller. I remember the first *mielga* I saw—no bigger than mutton breast, it was." However, the herders in this region use different sounds to guide their reindeer. The calls are different.

Ándom Ovllá sometimes wonders how Ristiinná can keep standing as solid as a cliff, despite the lashing of the waves. He's kept a weather eye on her. He was the one who decided to move the family, after all. Although she never wanted to come here, he's never once seen her lose her temper.

"She never says I was crazy for deciding to come here, never. I thought, she'll take me to task soon enough, but she hasn't. She's sad, no doubt about it, but she won't tell me how she's feeling. She bears her troubles alone." If Ándom Ovllá remarks on her silence, she replies that he, by contrast, would die if he had no one to talk to.

From time to time Márjá and Ristiinná work side by side with the other women, weaving, sewing, and spinning thread from reindeer sinews. They put the coffee pot on the fire unasked when the others turn up. The evenings are so dark down here: there's no sunlight for evening needlework. Once Ristiinná has finished winding shoe bands around the ankles of her brood, fed them all, and washed the dishes so that everything will be clean when they wake up, she falls soundly asleep. Looking back at the early days, even she is taken aback. There's no longer any time to think, the days and nights follow each other so fast. "What with sewing all those clothes and shoes, I had so much on my hands that there was never a moment to feel lonely, as I'd expected."

Márjá clambers up onto the *goahti* to rearrange the fabric around the smoke vent. Before going to bed, she watches the sparks dance out of the *reahpen* into the darkness. The days have grown shorter, and soon it will be time to travel eastward again. She doesn't know a soul in these parts and isn't sure where they can find lodgings. There must be bakehouses and vacant rooms available somewhere in exchange for a little money or a reindeer for slaughter. If anyone's prepared to have them as tenants, that is. It will all work out in the long term; it has to. This country will be lighter come the spring. Maybe they'll have a peat *goahti* of their own by next summer. Then she'll make a cupboard out of sugar boxes, and she'll have a table with an olive-green waxed cloth. Have pictures tacked on the beams of the *goahti*. But first of all she and Gusttu Bierar need to know if they can stay here with the others, or if they have to travel onward to the herding community chosen by the powers that be.

Gusttu Bierar and Márjá have received a letter from Lapp Bailiff Erik Malmström, a typewritten document addressed to "the Lapp Per Gustavsson Idivuoma." They are to receive 312 kronor and 50 öre, the last installment of their travel allowance. They will also receive a small sum to pay their guide. The tone of the letter suggests that the Lapp bailiff is satisfied: maybe that means they can stay where they are now?

"Finally, I should like to wish you every happiness and success in your new place of residence. Good luck!"

D. 45/8   N:r 95.

fogden i norrbottens
södra distrikt.

Till lappmannen Per Gustafsson Idivuoma,

Murjek.

Med anledning av dagens telefonsamtal översändes härjämte
i postanvisning till Eder sammanlagt trehundratolv (312) kronor
50 öre, utgörande dels 1/4-del av Eder tillkommande flyttningsbidrag, dels ock Anders Utsi tillkommande lotsersättning. Av
flyttningsbidraget har Ni ännu att fordra 142 kronor 50 öre.
Dessa medel äro emellertid innestående hos lappfogden Österberg,
och som denne för närvarande är sjukledig, kan Ni icke nu få
dessa penningar. Han återkommer till Luleå den 1 april, och
då skall jag säga till åt honom, att han skickar Edernbeloppet.

Tvenne kvittoblanketter bifogas. Kvittot å 112 kronor 50
öre skall undertecknas av Eder själv; kvittot å 200 kronor av
Anders Utsi. Var vänlig skicka mig kvittona, så fort Ni erhållit Utsis underskrift.

Till slut får jag önska Eder all lycka och välgång på Eder
nya vistelseort. Lycka till!

Luleå den 26 mars 1932.

"I do think about the north sometimes, about what every-day life was like there . . . Still, I suppose in the long term we did the right thing coming down here. But the authorities should have been more humane in the way they managed it, that I will say . . . And what about the people already living here who weren't asked their opinion and weren't told what was going to happen? They had people with different herding methods settling in their region. I can understand how they felt, it couldn't have been easy."

Is this home for you?

"Yes, it is . . . Mind you, we still have some of our roots up north. Down here it's just us, no one else. We had no grandpa or grandma on either side of the family, no aunts on my dad's side, no cousins. It was just our parents, no one else. Like pulling blinds down behind you, it was. I missed having family around me, even though we knew they were up there somewhere . . .

Our children, though, they feel quite differently about what counts as home. I'm fairly sure of that."

Ándom Ovllá Stiinná
Stina Andersson Omma,
daughter of Ándom Ovllá and Ristiinná

167

"We were born up north, the lot of us. Elise was the last one who was born in Skibotn. I was born in Mertajärvi, on the slopes of Mount Pekko. The Márggut 'maternity clinic' . . . They were kind people. Picture it—ten families or so, with their dogs, all in the same room. The floor was so packed, we were like canned herrings. The whole Márggut family lived in the same house.

I wasn't quite full-grown when we arrived here, but nearly. I was fourteen. Joined in with everything. We were strong skiers back then; we could ski for days at a time. *Hearrá sivdnit!* Good God! We used to ski behind the herd, alongside the *ráidu* that carried our *goahti*. It all went well; my parents were tough herding folk, they had what it took to work with reindeer. We traveled straight from Rostu to Balvatn . . . We had such a good life in Rostu—if only they'd let us be.

They were banished, that's what it comes down to, *isá ja joná eahki.* We tried for several years to get permission to go back to Sweden, to Árjepluovve or Johkamohki, but they wouldn't let us back in. They said there was no room. We were stateless. Our papers had gone missing. *Neavrri eŋgelat.* Angels of the Devil. It was shabby all right, the way they treated our parents. They didn't want to come here—they had a home, after all . . . But Sámi people back then were so afraid of officialdom. They thought they had to do as they were told. We couldn't stand up against them . . . That's just the way things were."

Máreha Biette Biera / Unna Bieraš
Per Blind, forcibly relocated in 1949 from
Geaggánvuopmi to Balvatn, Norway

Anders Georg Winka

Biito Biera

Petrus Johansson

Andom ovllä

stur elle

nihtel Biera Andde

Jóhkotnjárga

Sá Nir

12

Oappát ja vieljat
Last

They have dug out a gravel path leading up toward the mountain. It wasn't here last time. The excavated earth lies in heaps. Roots stick up through the peat.

I wander dry-shod over the bog. Scarcely any rain has fallen over the summer: the tussocks of scrub crackle with dryness, and the cloudberry flowers have closed.

I lose the path but head for the slope where it usually reappears. Behind me lies the city of Tromsø. If everything goes according to plan, much of this mountainside will be given over to alpine skiing facilities, conveniently located near the city, with slalom courses and chalets. The hotel is to be built just where the dwellings highest up on the slopes of Rávdnevággi once stood. I've tried to work out whether this is close to where our family lived, but I shall never know. None of the elders can remember now who lived where.

I'm wearing the belt *áhkku* gave me, woven from red, white, and blue strands of wool by an elderly woman in Gárasavvon. I asked my grandmother who she was. She knows your patterns, said *áhkku*, and the belt will be a gift to you. As I walk through the birch forest, my *gákti*, with its simple, old-fashioned zigzag bands, flaps about my legs in the breeze.

Sitting on a ledge with a view out over the valley, I draw my knees up toward my stomach, my wrist brushing sprigs of scrub that leave scratches as white and fine as spindly roots on my dry skin. I've begun to grasp that this is as close as I'll get.

"You can get to know the land, but it's harder with people," said Ánne Márjá, speaking of her family's forced displacement. "Only time will tell whether you've been blessed with a strong constitution."

Márggu Ántte Jouná, who settled permanently in the Sámi herding community of Vilhelmina södra (south) in 1960, said he had no energy left to travel any farther.

Although Dillá-*muore* was never one to grieve openly over her forced displacement, her family suffered because they never stopped moving from one place to another. Until the 1970s, the water in the Áhkájávvre reservoir was raised step by step, drowning their dwelling places. Their *goahtis* were pulled down and the family rebuilt them, time and again.

Biito Biera abandoned reindeer husbandry, married, and settled in one place for good. His home still contains all the belongings they packed into the sleds and brought down from the north.

Ándom Ovllá didn't want to look back. "I've never had any cause for regret; that's the truth of it," he said about his move to Västerbotten.

"But it was a long way up to Tromsø." His Ristiinná never stopped missing their old home.

In the mid-1930s, Márjá and Gusttu Bierar were finally authorized to stay in Umbyn for good. They didn't need to travel any farther. They built their own peat *goahti* in Striima, but in 1946 Gusttu Bierar died suddenly. Márjá got help with transporting her reindeer by rail and returning to the north.

The Skum family settled in the hamlet of Gávtsjávrrie (Ammarnäs). They battled poverty for many years but managed to build up their reindeer herd again.

I have traveled around to visit their children and grandchildren and hand over pictures, recordings, and documents from Lapp bailiffs. The last person I called on was Lásse Kemi in Nattavaara. Though well into his nineties, Lásse still lives on his own in his red house. He usually has instant coffee at the ready for guests, but this time he remarks that "the years have taken their toll." He lacks the energy to tell any more stories; his memory is failing. I hand him the photographs I brought, and we shake hands. Lásse says he's glad that at least one person has "drawn attention to that migration." Sitting silently on the steps outside his home, he adds: "The things that happen to us . . . it's hard."

These families are among the approximately three hundred people forcibly displaced between 1919 and 1932. But Sweden didn't stop forcibly displacing Sámi people from one herding community to another until the 1950s. Other families, living in the mountains of Jåhkåmåhkke and elsewhere, were displaced to make room for the people relocated to their community. Although the wounds opened by the resultant conflicts have healed in some places, in others they remain as deep as ever. Legal cases arising from the forced relocations are tearing Sámi society apart from within, making it impossible to go forward, to feel truly at home.

In this respect, the Swedish story matches a pattern familiar to Indigenous peoples the world over. In Australia, Aboriginal children are forcibly taken into care, while in Kalaalit Nunaat, Inuit people have been forcibly interned. In the United States, the routes traveled by the Cherokee and other nations are known as the Trail of Tears. The transgenerational trauma of Indigenous peoples is hardly ever documented in history books. In Sweden, too, Sámi history is considered to be a Sámi matter, not an integral part of Swedish history. In the Norwegian part of Sápmi, the story told in this book is seen as being about "the Swedish Sámi." It isn't thought relevant to Norwegians either.

If I close my eyes, I can see the *goahti* in the black-and-white photograph. Risten sits in front of it, with *váre*'s youngest sister in her arms. The photograph was taken a few years before their forced displacement. I'll never know exactly what happened during those years, but now I understand a little more about what was broken and silenced.

What would I have done if I'd been the one who was here for the last time? If I had known I would never return? Maybe I would have raised both hands to the birch trees and laid my cheek against the grassy shore of Hoggebohtu, turned toward Bealčán, given thanks to the hills around Suvigorsa. Dipping a hand in the cold spring at the bottom of the slope, I pull out a rough, uneven pebble. Blue-black-gray in color, it would fit in the palm of a child's hand. I drive home via Gilbbesjávri and lay the pebble in my kitchen window. Whenever I touch it, its unchanging coldness reminds me of the sea.

Now I shall stop weaving this narrative and hand the threads over to others. The gap in Sweden's history leaves ample space to weave our own patterns, in a voice that was never available to those who preceded us. In an interview with MajLis Skaltje, Iŋá-*muore váidni* said that the land would pass on our thanks to those coming after us. I believe it will also receive our thanks to those who lived before us. Hardly any of the elders in this book are still alive to continue telling their stories.

May the rocks echo with their joik.

"We remember how we joiked that last fall. There was liquor, and we made a fire and sent the reindeer herd off to the Swedish side of the border, while we stayed on for a celebration. We thanked Norway and its high peaks, the sea, the boats, the people. Some wept. We thanked the fine mountains where we'd thrived with our reindeer. We gave thanks to everything. And I don't believe we'll ever return . . . May the rocks of Norway echo with our joiks, echo with our thanks, and pass them on to future generations."

Defá Biette Iŋgá
Inga Idivuoma, who heard stories about the last fall her
parents spent in Norway before they were forcibly displaced

Josrvaid siida

Giittán
Acknowledgments

Thank you to all of you who told me your stories. I hope I have done them full justice. The text is based both on my own interviews and on conversations recorded by Inger Egemyr Blind *váidni*, Lars Valkeapää *váidni*, MajLis Skaltje, Olavi Korhonen, Gertrude Hanes, Per-Ola Utsi, Susanna Jannok Porsbo, and Kristina Skum. I am immensely grateful to you all. I also thank my father, Nils-Gustav Labba; John Erling Utsi; and, especially, Kristina Utsi Boine, who shared her work with me. This book belongs to all of you, too. Thank you, Johannes Marainen, for all the work you have done and continue to do. This book would never have been written without your *Karesuando sameslakter* (The Sámi Families of Karesuando). Johannes Marainen, Patrik Lantto, Dikka Storm, Stine Benedicte Sveen, and Ivar Björklund also helped paint the historical background to the stories told here. Thank you so much, Pia Sjögren, Åsa Nordin Jonsson, Gunilla Bergmark, and Henrik Sjöberg, for reading the text and making improvements. Nina Ulmaja, I thank you particularly for the sensitivity you brought to depicting joiks and silence, mountain plateaus and people. I am so glad you created the book's design. Most of all, Birgitta Östlund Weisglass, I thank you for freeing me from my *šielmma*, the stumbling block I had created.

Olles váimmuin giittán áhči ja enná go leahppi áŋgirit čuvvon mu mohkiid, Ol-Duommá, Nigo, Mihkkal Joná, Ánne Elise—eallima ovddas.

In addition to interviews, this book is based on documents and sound recordings from the Dialect and Folklore Archive of the Swedish Institute for Language and Folklore; the University Museum of Tromsø; Ájtte, the Swedish Mountain and Sámi Museum; the Lapp Bailiff Archive and the Church Archive, within the National Archives of Sweden; the Museum of Västerbotten; the Silver Museum; the Nordic Museum; the National Library of Sweden; the Swedish Meteorological and Hydrological Institute, SMHI; eKlima; legal texts; and research, documentation, and newspaper articles about forced relocations and cross-border reindeer husbandry in Sweden and Norway.

Appendix
Translated Documents

Swedish Law on the Number of Reindeer in Sámi Communities, 1925 (Chapter 6)

Document from the Lapp Bailiff Archive, Regional Archive, Härnösand.

COMPILATION OF SWEDISH LEGAL STATUTES
1925
No. 181–183.
Printed on 18th June

No. 181
Law
(Title and date to be announced in church)
concerning the reduction, in certain cases, of the number of reindeer within a Lapp herding community
issued at Stockholm Castle, 6th June 1925

We, Gustaf, by the grace of God King of Sweden, the Goths and the Wends, hereupon make known that We, together with the Parliament of Sweden, hereby rescind Section 8 of the Law of 1 July 1898 (No. 66) on the right of the Swedish Lapps to reindeer pasturage in Sweden, and order as follows:

Section 1

1. If the reindeer within a Lapp herding community are found to be so numerous that the pastureland available must be deemed inadequate or the said reindeer are causing significant damage, and if there are reindeer within the said Lapp herding district that belong to non-Lapps, the County Administrative Board may, after giving the Lapps a hearing, order that as many reindeer as may be deemed necessary for

the purpose be removed from the Lapp herding community within a specified period of time, and that those reindeer be dealt with by the official responsible within the Lapp herding community and sold either as livestock or after slaughter at the owner's expense. More detailed provisions on how this is to be accomplished shall be announced by the County Administrative Board, on whom it is thus incumbent to protect the rights and interests of individual reindeer owners, as far as possible, and to ensure that the livelihoods of reindeer-herding Lapps are not disproportionately affected.

2. If there are still too many reindeer left after any reindeer that are the property of non-Lapps have been removed from the Lapp herding district in accordance with subsection 1., the County Administrative Board may, after giving a hearing to the Lapps of both the Lapp herding community in question and the Lapp community to which such Lapps may be assigned, assign one or more Lapps to another Lapp community with sufficient capacity, where they may be relocated without undue inconvenience. In so doing, the County Administrative Board shall ensure that Lapps who have long belonged to a Lapp herding community or had the right to pasturage for their reindeer within its district, or whose ancestors were part of the said community or held such rights, shall not be assigned to a different Lapp herding community against their will, unless there is a particular reason to do so.

Denial of Funds to Iŋggá Biette (Per Tomasson Skum) from the Governor of Norrbotten, 1932 (Chapter 9)

The County Administrative Board rejects Iŋggá Biette's request for financial assistance after the family has lost a large part of their reindeer herd during their forced relocation. Document from the Lapp Bailiff Archive, Regional Archive, Härnösand.

County Governor
County of Norrbotten
County Secretariat No. L. 11/28

Folio 184 No. 239
Received by the Office of the Lapp Bailiff, Umeå, 29 December 1932

To the Lapp Bailiff of the County of Västerbotten.

Concerning the request submitted by Per Tomasson Skum, of the Lapp herding community of Gran, for a certain amount of financial assistance.

The request concerns an application for a grant to cover the rounding up and transfer to Västerbotten of reindeer that did not follow the rest of the herd on its departure from Gällivare. The state has already been obliged to spend considerable sums above and beyond the transfer grant established by His Royal Majesty, with which other Lapps in similar circumstances have had to content themselves, on the transfer to Västerbotten of Skum, his household, his household goods, and his reindeer. In view of the above, and since it appears rather uncertain that Skum would be able to round up and transfer the remaining reindeer with the help of any allowance that might be granted, the County Administrative Board is of the opinion that there should be no question of any further state expenditure in this case. Moreover, driving a comparatively small number of reindeer over such a long distance is liable to prove a somewhat fruitless enterprise, since reindeer have a well-known penchant for returning to their former home region. In the view of the County Administrative Board, the most appropriate solution is therefore for Skum to authorize the Lapp Authority's officials to sell those of his reindeer that remain in the county, after which he can use the proceeds of the sale to purchase reindeer in the district where he now resides. He will not be required to cover the costs incurred in rounding up and selling off the reindeer. The above details are furnished for your information and kind attention, as well as for Skum's information.

Luleå, County Secretariat, 27 December 1932.

Correspondence to King Gustaf V of Sweden from Johan Nilsson Kemi and Nikolaus [Nils] Nilsson Kemi, 1929 (Chapter 10)

To the King
4/4.1929

Having learned from the newspapers that the Administrative Board of the County of Norrbotten has issued a statement concerning our legal action against our forced relocation, we hereby entreat you once more with the deepest humility, as follows. Firstly, we humbly request leave to remain in the summering grounds where both we and our reindeer grew to adulthood, as previously mentioned. Secondly, should that be impossible, we request permission to live in the Wittangi herding community of forest Lapps, situated between Annisjoki and the Lainioälven River, east of the road linking Soppero and Wittangi.

Because other Lapps like ourselves are permitted to live there without there being any over-crowding, <u>even though they are not forest Lapps by origin</u>, such as the Mangi brothers, whose father, like our father Nils Mikkelsen Kemi, was once a mountain Lapp and who moved to live in the forest at the same time as our father, some 25 years ago. It feels rather personal when certain people are subject to a different law from that which is applied to others.

<u>And thirdly,</u> if that is not possible either, we request permission to follow in our father's footsteps and to live as mountain Lapps in <u>the Lapp herding community of Talma</u> in the parish of Jukkasjärvi, migrating to Norway during the summer.

We are putting forward the above proposal in all humility, in the hope that our long and difficult journey to Stockholm may not have been in vain.

Soppero, 4 April 1929
Your humble servants
Johan Nilsson Kemi   Nikolaus Nilsson Kemi

From *Dagens Nyheter* (national Swedish newspaper), 7 January 1929 (Chapter 10)

N. F. Johansson and J. Nilsson

Two Vittangi Lapps Plead for Their Reindeer Pasturage and Entreat the King's Mercy

Stockholm currently has two Lapp visitors who have made the long journey from Vittangi in the County of Norrbotten for the purpose of a personal audience with the King about a complex issue concerning reindeer pasturage. The two men began their journey early on Thursday morning, at a temperature of minus 20 degrees Celsius, arriving on Saturday evening at Stockholm's Central Station, in a fog as dense as a London pea-souper. They picked their way gingerly in their Lapp shoes through the city's ice-glazed streets to their lodgings.

The two travelers are Johan Nilsson-Kemi, a forest Lapp from the far-flung parish of Vittangi, and the settler and lawyer N. F. Johansson, a

Lapp from the same district as the aforesaid, who is his legal represent-ative and will act as his interpreter and spokesman at the audience with the King. The issue is as follows. Johan Nilsson-Kemi, who, incidentally, speaks only Lappish and Finnish, and his brother Nikolaus, the joint owners of three hundred reindeer, who have spent their entire lives, as settled forest Lapps, within an area of about ten square kilometers in the parish of Vittangi, have been instructed by the Lapp bailiff responsible, the Administrative Board of the County of Norrbotten, and the Govern-ment, to relocate to a different district to which they have been assigned, located in the parish of Gällivare. However, it is extremely hard for the two Lapps to accept this decision . . .

From *Haparandabladet* (Swedish regional newspaper), 14 March 1931 (Chapter 10)

The Kemi Brothers' Reindeer Herd: A Deplorable Quandary

A conflict that has dragged on for four years is now finally about to be resolved. It concerns the reindeer owned by the Kemi brothers, Nikolaus and Johan. Following a decision by the County Administrative Board, these were supposed to be moved in March 1927 from the overcrowded grazing land of the Soppero district to the Lapp herding community of Gällivare, which has significantly more pasture available. It is common knowledge that the Kemi brothers, who have in fact stayed on illegally in Soppero for a good ten years, have come up with all kinds of pretexts in defiance of the decision to relocate them. One of them even had an audience with the King a few years ago.

According to the local Lapp Bailiff Pappila, the reindeer in ques-tion have finally been transferred to the parish of Gällivare by the Lapp inspectors, but the Kemi brothers have refused to accompany their herd. This is the first case in which it has been necessary to relocate reindeer under duress. It will, however, have serious material consequences for the stubborn Kemi brothers, as the costs of relocation are in excess of 1,000 kronor. The County Administrative Board has decreed that this sum is to be raised next week by selling off the requisite number of the brothers' reindeer. The herd currently numbers over 180 fine animals.

Correspondence to Gusttu Bierar (Per Gustafsson Idivuoma) from the Acting Lapp Bailiff of Norrbotten, 1932 (Chapter 11)

Letter sent to Gusttu Bierar after he had arrived at his "place of residence." Document from the Lapp Bailiff Archive, Regional Archive, Härnösand.

Lapp Bailiff for the southern district of the County of Norrbotten.

To the Lapp Per Gustafsson Idivuoma, <u>Murjek</u>

Further to today's telephone conversation, I am sending you herewith, by postal order, a total of three hundred and twelve (312) kronor and 50 öre, composing one-quarter of the travel allowance allotted to you plus the fee due to Anders Utsi as guide. The sum outstanding from your travel allowance is 142 kronor and 50 öre. However, these funds are held by Lapp Bailiff Österberg, and since he is sick at the moment the sum cannot be paid to you for the time being. Mr. Österberg is due to return to Luleå on 1 April, and I shall ask him to send you the money then.

Please find enclosed two receipts: one for the sum of 112 kronor and 50 öre, to be signed by you, and another for 200 kronor, to be signed by Anders Utsi. Kindly return these receipts to me once you have obtained Utsi's signature.

Finally, I should like to wish you every happiness and success in your new place of residence. Good luck!

Luleå, 26 March 1932.

[*signature*]

Acting Lapp Bailiff

186

Glossary

These North Sámi terms are defined according to their use in this book.

áddjá grandfather

áhče father

áhkku grandmother

áiti storehouse

árran fireplace or hearth in the middle of a Sámi dwelling (*goahti*), usually formed by a ring of stones

asttahát sticks used to poke the open fire

bággojohtin forced displacement, forced relocation

bealljegoahti arch-beamed *goahti* (Swedish, *bågstångkåta*)

bearrjas length of fabric used to cover the wind side of a *goahti*'s smoke vent

beaska fur garment

birget surviving and coping

boaššu the area at the back of a *goahti,* opposite the door, where food and cooking utensils are stored; a sacred place that is not to be entered

buoggi cache or storehouse above the ground, where migrating Sámi could store belongings to be retrieved later in the year

čogogoahti small tent used when traveling

cuipi peak of a hat or cap worn by Sámi men

dovgosat padding for a pack saddle

eidde mother (from the Karesuando region and areas bordering Finland)

gáhkku flat, round bread baked over an open fire

gákti Sámi tunic worn by men and women, typically blue with red and yellow trim

geres sled pulled by reindeer; a *ráidu* (reindeer caravan) is formed by a number of *geres*

gietkka portable cradle that can be carried by a person or by a pack reindeer in a *ráidu*

gietkkamánát babies small enough to be carried in a cradle

giisá (plural, **giissáid**) small box for transporting items of value when traveling by reindeer caravan

giitos many thanks

gilis mixture of blood, flour, sinews, bone, etc., used to feed dogs

gintalbeaivi Candlemas, a Christian feast day celebrated on 2 February

goahtegeres sled to transport the *goahti*

goahti traditional Sámi home: a rounded hut built of stones and turf, especially peat; could also refer to a tent of fabric or hide on a wooden frame, used during seasonal migrations

goavvi a harsh winter; a lean year

gohppogisá chest or box to transport china cups during seasonal migrations

hode Lapp bailiff (Swedish, *lappfogde*), a state official with far-reaching powers over Sámi herding communities and reindeer husbandry in a given region

holga drying rack made of the trunks of birches or other trees, used to air bedclothes and hang items outside the home

horstaseahkat sackcloth bags

ipmil sivdnit may the Lord bless us

isá father (from the Karesuando region and areas bordering Finland)

isidát *siida* leaders

joik Sámi vocal music, often addressed to features of the landscape, such as mountains, hills, or lakes, or to animals or people; also, to sing in this manner: one is said to joik a person or animal or a feature of the landscape when singing to express feelings about them

juoigalaš fond of and good at joiking

leanska county police officer, comparable to a U.S. sheriff (Swedish, *länsman*)

liidni neckerchief, scarf

loaidu a *goahti* divided into two sides, where people sat or lay down

luohti a particular kind of joik

máhearra county governor in Sweden (Swedish, *landshövding*)

márjjábeaivvit St. Mary's Day (near the end of March)

máttaráddjá great-grandfather

máttaráhkku great-grandmother

mielga reindeer breast (cut of meat)

muitalit to tell, to recount

muitit to remember, to recall

muore a mature woman with a certain standing; grandmother; can be attached to a person's name, e.g., Dillá-*muore*

nuvttahat Sámi shoes made of reindeer hide, with upturned toes ("beak shoes")

oappát ja vieljat brothers and sisters

oarjelsadji a Southern Sámi settlement

ohca neck opening in a Sámi tunic (*gákti*)

ráffedorka additional garment worn over a hide garment

rággas/rákkas individual "tent" of thin cotton, used inside a *goahti* at night to add warmth in winter, to keep mosquitoes away in summer, and to provide privacy

ráidu caravan of interlinked Sámi sleds drawn by draft reindeer, typically geldings

rátnu thick woolen hanging or blanket

reahpen vent in the center of a *goahti* to let out the smoke from the central fireplace

rissla high-sided sledge pulled by horses or reindeer, used to transport people

roavgu fleece that serves as bedding

Sápmi the region inhabited by Sámi people (extending through northern Norway, Sweden, Finland, and the Kola Peninsula of northwestern Russia)

sápmi Sámi people

šielbma threshold on the way into a *goahti*

siessá father's sister

siida local Sámi community based on family ties; also a reindeer grazing area used by that community

siidaisit head of a *siida*

sirdolaččat displaced Sámi people; a word used by the first people forced to relocate

sivnnar Sámi name for a Lapp inspector (Swedish, *lapptillsynings-man*). These inspectors were responsible for carrying out practical tasks at the local level, under the auspices of the regional Lapp bailiff, the *lappfogde.*

skoaddu fog

soggi the part of the *goahti* right next to the tent fabric (or the walls, in the case of a peat *goahti*), where bedclothes and other belongings were kept

spagát reindeer saddle with two projections at the front for the rider to hold on to; used by small children no longer able to travel in a *gietkka* but not yet old enough to walk during seasonal migrations

stállu ogre-like mythical character believed to attack and eat Sámi people

stuoranjárgajohtti inhabitant of Stuoranjárga (the Troms Peninsula, Norway)

sundi Lapp bailiff (see *hode*)

suohpan lasso, used to lasso reindeer. A tangled lasso was believed to bode ill for a forthcoming childbirth, suggesting that the umbilical cord might become entangled.

suohpangiehta a person skilled in lassoing reindeer; a lasso hand

suoidnevierra dried sedge (used to stuff shoes and keep out the cold), woven into a wreath for ease of storage and transport. Children wore these wreaths on their heads like halos, pretending to be St. Lucia. St. Lucia's Day is a Swedish feast day on 13 December, when St. Lucia, wearing a crown of candles, leads processions of children.

unna reaŋga young hired boy or hired hand

váidni a person who has passed away; can be appended to a name, e.g., Lars Valkeapää *váidni* (the late Lars Valkeapää)

váre grandfather

verdde host or foster family; settled family engaged in regular trade with a Sámi family

vuoddaga (plural, **vuoddagat**) colorful woven bands or bindings for the lower leg (similar to puttees), designed to keep snow and rain out of shoes; usually translated as "shoe bands"

Sámi Geographical Names

Aartege Artfjället (Swedish), a massif near Strimasund. Aartege is the South Sámi name.

Árjepluovve Arjeplog (town, Sweden); "Árjeploug" in older documents.

Duortnosjávri Torneträsk (lake, Sweden); *jávri* is North Sámi for "lake"

Gáranasvuotna Ramsfjorden (fjord, Norway)

Gárasavvon Karesuando (town, Sweden)

Giebnegáisi Kebnekaise (Sweden's highest mountain)

Gilbbesjávri Kilpisjärvi (village, Finland)

Giron Kiruna (town, Sweden)

Guovdageaidnu Kautokeino (village, Norway)

Ittonjárga Lyngen (peninsula, Norway); *njárga* is North Sámi for "peninsula"

Jåhkåmåhkke/Johkamohki Jokkmokk (town, Sweden)

Jáhkotnjárgga Malangshalvøya (peninsula, Norway)

Jiellevárre Gällivare (town, Sweden)

Nearvá Mertajärvi (Sweden)

Rávdjevággi Finnheia (area of the Norwegian island of Kvaløya/ Sállir)

Rijtjem Ritsem (Sweden)

Romsa Tromsø (city, Norway)

Romsavággi/Romsavákki Tromsdalen (valley, Norway)

Rostu Rostu (hilly area west of Karesuando, Sweden)

Sállir Kvaløya (island, Norway)

Sážža Senja (island, Norway)

Sohppar Soppero (village, Sweden)

Striima Strimasund (hamlet, Sweden)

Stuoranjárga Troms (peninsula, Norway)

Suorssá Sorsele (village, Sweden)

Photography Captions and Credits

Joiks

front endpapers Johan Turi, *Muitalus sámiid birra*, ed. Mikael Svonni, *Sámi academica* 3, ed. Harald Gaski (Karasjok: ČálliidLágádus, 2010), 90; and Johan Turi, *An Account of the Sámi: A Translation of Muitalus sámiid birra, Based on the Sámi Original*, trans. Thomas A. DuBois (Karasjok: ČálliidLágádus, 2012), 96. Courtesy of Thomas A. Dubois.

page v *The Sun, My Father*, trans. Ralph Salisbury, Lars Nordström, and Harald Gaski (Guovdageaidnu [Kautokeino]: DAT, 1988). Courtesy of Harald Gaski.

page 46 Paulus Utsi, from *Don čanat mu alccesat*, trans. Thomas A. DuBois and Harald Gaski (Guovdageaidnu [Kautokeino]: DAT, 1992), 91.

page 84 Translated by Thomas A. DuBois and Harald Gaski.

page 132 Translated by Thomas A. DuBois and Harald Gaski with permission from a descendant of Iŋggá Biette.

page 148 Translated by Thomas A. DuBois and Harald Gaski.

Illustrations

front endpaper Photograph: Carl-Johan Utsi.

front inside endpaper The path from Hoggebohtu to Rávdnjevággi on the island of Sállir (Kvaløya), Norway. Photograph: Elin Anna Labba.

back endpapers Reindeer calving grounds on the Ittonjárga (Lyngen) peninsula, Norway. Photograph: Elin Anna Labba.

pages ii–iii In the streets of Romsa (Tromsø), Norway. On the way to church, perhaps? Photograph from the Høegh Collection / Perspektivet Museum (Tromsø).

page viii The church in Gárasavvon (Karesuando), Sweden, 1908. Everyone would gather here during the main religious festivals, such as Christmas, Easter, and *márjjábeaivvit* (St. Mary's Day) at the end of March. Photograph: Emilie Demant Hatt, Arctic University Museum of Norway (Tromsø).

page x Suorgi (Kittdalen). Ancient migration trail between summer and winter pastureland, near the present Swedish–Norwegian border. Photograph: H. A. Vinje, Arctic University Museum of Norway (Tromsø).

page 3 *Váhkara* Risten with her children Márge and Joná. She holds the youngest child, who lived only a few years. Photograph: Eliel Lagercrantz, Museovirasto— Finnish National Board of Antiquities.

page 5 Those who don't need to accompany the reindeer herd cross the fjord by ferry, holding their puppies and children. Photograph from the Høegh Collection / Perspektivet Museum (Tromsø).

page 6 Rávdjie (Straumen), near the point where the reindeer swam over to the island of Sállir (Kvaløya) from the mainland. Photograph: Olaus Solberg, Arctic University Museum of Norway (Tromsø).

pages 10–11 Reindeer on spring migration toward summer pastures. Photograph: Carl-Johan Utsi.

page 12 A family outside their *goahti* on the island of Sážžá (Senja), Norway, during one of their last summers in their summer home. Photograph: Ossian Elgström, Nordic Museum (Stockholm).

page 19 Guhtur Omma holds a female reindeer still while Ánne Márjá Omma milks her, in the Bárká, Tuorpon, herding community, where the couple was forcibly relocated. Photograph: Bert Persson.

page 25 Inside the Palopää family's *goahti*, in their wintering grounds. It may be Sunday: a woman is reading the Bible. Photograph: Ossian Elgström, Nordic Museum (Stockholm).

pages 26–27 The Heaikka family's application for relocation. The signature *NTH* is the only part of the document written by a family member; everything else was written by the Lapp Authority. Document from the Lapp Bailiff Archive, Regional Archive, Härnösand (Sweden).

page 28 Márggu Ántte Nilsá *(left)* and his brother Márggu Ánte Jouná *(right)*, Suorvvá, 1920. One of the few photographs taken on the journey south. Photograph: Hjalmar Falk, Nordic Museum (Stockholm).

page 33 Best friends Gár Ántte Biret, Márggu Biera Elle, and Márggu Biera Márja in Suorvvá, March 1920. Photograph: Hjalmar Falk, Nordic Museum (Stockholm).

pages 36–37 Church register of relocated Sámi people, Karesuando (Gárasavvon), 1921. Swedish National Archives.

page 40 Sámi people on their way home after a meeting with the Lapp bailiff in Árjepluovve (Arjeplog), Sweden, 1924. Photograph: Axel Svensson, Silver Museum Archive.

page 45 Letter of thanks from relocated people, which Márggu Ántte Jouná said he had never written. Document from the Lapp Bailiff Archive, Regional Archive, Härnösand.

pages 46–47 Sirges, or "Sirkkis," as Paulus Utsi writes in his poem from 1966 about the Sámi herding community of that name. Photograph: Carl-Johan Utsi, taken from Rávdooajvve.

page 48 Dillá-*muore* (Margareta Utsi) in her peat *goahti* in Vájsáluokta. One of the boys hides his face in the bedclothes. Privately owned photograph.

page 55 The Utsi family in Ivgomuotki (Lyngseidet), Norway, a few years before their forced relocation. Photograph: Ossian Elgström, Nordic Museum (Stockholm).

page 57 View over Vájsáluokta and Boalnu from Áhkká after the lake had been dammed for the first time. Photograph: Ernst Manker, Nordic Museum (Stockholm).

page 58 Dillá-*muore* on the shore of Lake Áhkájávrre, 1956. Photograph from Paulus Utsi's memorial fund archive.

page 65 The Utsi family: Mihkel Biera, Biette, Mihkkal, Ándde, Jovnna, Lásse, Nigá, Bávlos, and Dillá. Photograph taken by the Gárasavvon (Karesuando) pastor; courtesy of Hjalmar Westenson.

page 66 Ándom Ovllá (Olof Andersson Omma) plays with his dog in Romssavággi (Tromsdalen), Norway, 1908. Photograph: Emilie Demant Hatt, Arctic University Museum of Norway (Tromsø).

page 67 Wedding photograph of Ándom Ovllá (Olof Andersson Omma) and Ristiinná (Kristina Omma), Tromsø, 1923. Privately owned photograph.

page 76 In a boat on the way to storekeepers in Romsa (Tromsø), Norway. Photograph: Arctic University Museum of Norway (Tromsø).

page 77 Girls walking to the Stuoranjárga (Troms) peninsula. Only the very youngest children were allowed to ride the pack reindeer. Photograph: Emilie Demant Hatt, Arctic University Museum of Norway (Tromsø).

pages 84–85 Joik sung by Biito Biera (Per Markus Bals), recorded by Kristina Utsi Boine. This is one of the few joiks about forced displacement that have been preserved. Photograph: Carl-Johan Utsi.

page 86 Reindeer corral in Ubmeje *tjeälddie* (the Sámi herding community of Umbyn). Photograph: Ernst Manker, Nordic Museum (Stockholm).

page 95 Photograph showing one of the first times that a herd was held in a corral in the herding community of Sirges while the reindeer were divided among their various owners, which was done in summer. This scene appears in the film *I fjällfolkets land* (In the Land of the Mountain Folk). Photograph: Erik Bergström.

page 101 A family on the move with their *ráidu*. The woman sits on a *geres* (a Sámi sled); she might hold a child in her arms. Photograph: Emilie Demant Hatt, Arctic University Museum of Norway (Tromsø).

page 103 Sámi herding community of Sirges, Gierkav, 1943. Photograph: Sture Björnström, Nordic Museum (Stockholm).

page 104 Márjá (Anna Maria Idivuoma) outside her peat *goahti* in Vájsáluokta. Lengths of wood were placed against the outside wall of the *goahti* to stop the family's goats from climbing on the roof. Photograph: Ethel Lindgren.

page 107 Gusttu Bierar (Per Gustavsson Idivuoma), 1937. He and Márjá finally managed to build a *goahti* of their own. Photograph: Göte Haglund, Museum of Västerbotten (Umeå, Sweden).

page 109 Márjá lays a *bearjjas* alongside the *goahti*'s smoke hole, to stop the wind from blowing smoke back into the tent. Photograph: Ernst Manker, Nordic Museum (Stockholm).

page 112 The Walkeapää family does laundry on the shore of Lake Áhkájávrre, 1940. Photograph: Ernst Manker, Nordic Museum (Stockholm).

pages 114–15 "I think that's my brother Biette, the one who drowned," says Elle Susá Nordqvist, née Walkeapää. The picture was taken on Lake Áhkájávrre in 1940. Photograph: Ernst Manker, Nordic Museum (Stockholm).

page 117 Johannes Labba, Ánne Labba, and Kristina Labba (*Joná, Ánne ja Risten*) on the steps of their new house in Porjus, Norrbotten (Sweden). The picture with the boats shows the family landing at Vájsaluokta in 1956. Photographs are privately owned.

page 120 Čuoigi Elle Gáren (Helena Skum) and Iŋggá Biette (Per Tomasson Skum), Vazáš (Vittangi), 1915. Iŋggá Biette holds their daughter Iŋger Ánna. Photograph: Borg Mesch, Kiruna municipality's picture collection.

page 123 Reindeer ear marks from Granbyn: south Sámi ear marks together with those of the Partapuoli and Skum families. Document from the Lapp Bailiff Archive, Regional Archive, Härnösand.

page 128 This photograph is thought to have been taken in 1926, on the day before the start of the forced relocation. Biette, Iŋggá Biette, Čuoigi Elle Gáren, and Johánas are seated on a *geres* in the village of Vittangi. Photograph: Ernst Klein, Nordic Museum (Stockholm).

page 131 From the family album. Iŋggá Biette Susánna (Susanna Andersson). Privately owned photograph.

page 136 Biret Ánne Kemi, Nils Kemi, and Lapp Bailiff Edvin Kangas, Lake Guobmujávrre, Muttos, 1950. "That Edvin Kangas again," said Lásse Kemi when he saw this photograph for the first time. Photograph: Ernst Manker, Nordic Museum (Stockholm).

page 138 The Kemi family's *goahti* alongside the marshland on the shores of Lake Guobmujávrre, Muttos, 1950. Photograph: Ernst Manker, Nordic Museum (Stockholm).

page 143 *Dagens Nyheter*, National Library of Sweden.

pages 148–49 Wintering grounds by the Rappo bog in Norrbotten, Sweden. Photograph: Carl-Johan Utsi.

page 150 Biret Ánne Kemi (Britta Johanna), the keen storyteller, at Lake Guobmujávrre, Norrbotten, Sweden, in 1950. Her husband, Nils, tried to register their reindeer in her name to avoid having to move to a different region or being forced to cull the herd, but that proved impossible. Photograph: Ernst Manker, Nordic Museum (Stockholm).

page 155 Sleds packed with belongings on their way westward. Photograph: Emilie Demant Hatt, Arctic University Museum of Norway (Tromsø).

page 156 Márjá (Anna Maria) Idivuoma, Striima (Strimasund), 1937. "She used to say it was so dark in Tärna," recalls her daughter, Ella Idivuoma Marklund. Photograph: Göte Haglund, Museum of Västerbotten (Umeå, Sweden).

page 159 Ristiinná (Kristina Omma), Striima (Strimasund), 1937. After she died, her husband, Ándom Ovllá, said he missed her terribly. Photograph: Göte Haglund, Museum of Västerbotten (Umeå, Sweden).

page 162 Ándom Ovllá Iŋgá (Inga Baer), in front of her *rággas* (anti-mosquito "tent") in the family's peat *goahti* in Striima (Strimasund), 1935. Iŋgá was the strongest of them all, and she loved working with reindeer. Photograph: Ernst Manker, Nordic Museum (Stockholm).

page 166 The Omma children (some of Ristiinná and Ándom Ovllá's children). According to younger sister Stina Omma, this picture shows Olle, Ella, Sire, and Anna. Striima (Strimasund), 1935. Photograph: Ernst Manker, Nordic Museum (Stockholm).

page 169 The first encounter between the new arrivals and the reindeer herders of Umbyn, 1931. Anders Georg Winka, Petrus Johansson, Per Markus Bals, Ella Blind, Olof Andersson Omma, and Anders Utsi. Photograph by an unknown photographer, Museum of Västerbotten (Umeå, Sweden).

page 170 Rávdnji (Straumen) on the island of Sállir (Kvaløya), Norway, 2018. Photograph: Elin Anna Labba.

page 175 Nutti Iŋgá's family: Iŋgá-*muore*, Olá, Márge, Johán, and Susánná. Privately owned photograph.

pages 176–77 Josvvaid *siida*, Kuhmunen *siida* (family group). Part of the family ended up farther south, while others remained in the north. Photograph: Ossian Elgström, Nordic Museum (Stockholm).

Elin Anna Labba is a journalist based in Saltdal (northern Norway) and Jokkmokk (northern Sweden), both within Sápmi. *The Rocks Will Echo Our Sorrow* was awarded the 2020 August Prize for best nonfiction book in Sweden and has been translated into six languages.

Fiona Graham is a British translator living in Belgium. She has worked as a linguist with the Dutch Foreign Ministry, the European Parliament, and the European Commission. She has translated six books, including Elisabeth Åsbrink's *1947: When Now Begins*.